THE AMATEUR METEOROLOGIST

Explorations and Investigations

by H. Michael Mogil and Barbara G. Levine

An Amateur Science Series Book
FRANKLIN WATTS
New York · Chicago · London · Toronto · Sydney

Library of Congress Cataloging-in-Publication Data

Mogil, H. Michael.
The amateur meteorologist : explorations and investigations / by
H. Michael Mogil and Barbara G. Levine.
p.   cm.—(An Amateur science series book)
Includes bibliographical references and index.
Summary: Presents activities and projects with which the amateur
meteorologist can explore the weather.
ISBN 0-531-11045-1
1. Meteorology—Observers' manuals—Juvenile literature.
2. Meteorology—Juvenile literature. [1. Weather.   2. Meteorology.
3. Science projects.]   I. Levine, Barbara G.   II. Series.
QC871.7.M64   1993
551.5—dc20   93-17506 CIP AC

Contents

Look, Listen, and Feel

Watch and feel the *weather!* Look at the clouds! Are they wispy or puffy? What colors are they? Is the weather hot or cold? humid or dry? Did you see any lightning or hear any thunder? What other weather sounds did you hear (for example, leaves rustling, wind whistling, rain falling)? Compare the color of the sky to what it was yesterday. Is it as blue? Has it rained or snowed recently? Did the rain puddle in some places but not in others? What about snowdrifts? What did you notice about the color of the snow after a few days? Have you ever touched dew or frost, or collected rain or snow?

Check on weather in the news. Examine the newspaper weather page and skim the entire newspaper for weather headlines or stories about the weather. Tune in to television and radio news and weather reports, too. Find out about significant weather happenings in your area, across the nation, and around the world. How did your weather observations compare to these weather events?

Meteorology is the scientific study of weather. Scientists trained in the study of the atmosphere are called *meteorologists.* Some meteorologists forecast the weather; others conduct scientific and computer simulations of global weather patterns and study how these patterns change; still others analyze the composition of the air we breathe, trying to understand the meteorological forces which contribute to air pollution.

Meteorologists collect weather *data*. Thermometers, barometers, anemometers, wind vanes, and rain gauges are among the tools they regularly use. Most of these instruments operate according to simple, easy-to-understand scientific principles and are easy to use. There are also several new types of weather instruments, such as satellite and radar. You'll read about all of these instruments—the old and the new alike—later in this book.

We are all interested in the weather because it constantly affects our lives. But meteorologists are people who carry that interest much further than the casual observer. They use scientific principles and methods to collect and analyze data in order to understand the nature and effects of weather. If you have that kind of interest in weather, this book can help you to become an amateur meteorologist. And you won't have to buy expensive professional-type instruments and equipment to measure the atmosphere. *The Amateur Meteorologist* will show you how to build your own weather instruments from materials you can find in your own home or that are easy to get elsewhere. The only instruments or equipment you might want to buy are a few thermometers, a kit to measure the acidity of rainfall, and some items which can be used to make better-quality instruments. Your newspaper and television can provide weather satellite and radar photographs and additional weather observations. If you are already a more experienced weather enthusiast—or when you get to be one—you will probably want to use more-precise equipment. We've listed some sources of professional-type weather instruments (see p. 125).

You can become an amateur meteorologist by making and recording weather observations, classifying the clouds you see, conducting weather experiments, and making weather forecasts. In doing so, you will begin to understand how and why weather happens. You will learn how to use meteorology to improve your personal comfort, safety, and economic well-being. For example, if you predict strong winds, your family might cancel a picnic outing. Why wash the family car when you know it is going to rain? The television weather forecast and your own observations can guide you in how to dress for the weather. You can leave that sweater at home if it's going to be a warm day.

Record your observations several times a day in a weather journal, just as Benjamin Franklin and Thomas Jefferson did in eighteenth-century colonial America. In your journal, include observations about cloud types, how the weather changed from morning to afternoon, and any interesting phenomena (for example, heavy snow, thunderstorms, strong winds, or rapid temperature changes). How did the weather affect your area (for example, roads closed due to flooding, traffic accidents caused by snow or fog)? How did the weather make you and your family feel?

You may not have experienced all of the weather events described in this book. However, as you grow older and visit new places, you will likely encounter many of them. Even if you don't, other family members may. When you talk with family members who live in other states, ask them about their weather and tell them about yours.

Weather is everywhere. It happens day and night, every day of the year. And it is constantly changing. This is true even in places where the weather conditions remain much the same for many consecutive days. Take advantage of this to experience weather and weather-related phenomena in your home, on vacation, when you drive around town, and every time you go outside.

But please be careful. Weather can be dangerous. Thunderstorms contain lightning, high winds, hail, and sometimes tornadoes. Winter storms are often accompanied by frigid temperatures and very strong winds. Hurricanes bring high winds and flooding.

Even tranquil weather can be dangerous. Sometimes, air may become filled with chemicals and pollutants, especially when winds only blow gently for several days. The sun, which is basically a friend, can also be very deadly. Its rays can burn our skin and damage our eyes in a short time. Even on cloudy days, ultraviolet rays from the sun can reach the Earth. Sky watching requires special care. Never look directly at the sun, even if you are wearing tinted or protective sunglasses.

Although many of the activities described in this book can be done safely by yourself, it's always a good idea to check with adults in your household or get their assistance. This is especially important when using electricity, fire, or other potentially hazardous materials.

A NOTE ON TEMPERATURE CONVERSIONS

As you work your way through the activities and projects that follow, use the following formulas to make temperature conversions:

$$°C = 5/9 \times (°F - 32)$$
$$°F = 9/5°C + 32$$

How to Collect and Interpret Weather Data

Now that you've begun to experience the weather, it's time to collect, tabulate, analyze, classify, and chart weather information. You'll also learn how to read a weather map and how to make your first weather forecasts. Be prepared to ask yourself questions, just as an investigative reporter or a detective might do.

WIND

Think about the *wind*. How does it affect us? Look for ways that the wind helps us (for example, by keeping a kite aloft, operating a windmill, cooling us on a hot summer day) and harms us (by blowing down trees, by making us feel even colder on a frigid winter day). Can you estimate the wind speed and direction using only your eyes and fingers and no instruments? You can compare your visual observations to that of an anemometer you will build soon and with the wind speed reported on local television or radio weather reports.

Beaufort Scale • The Beaufort scale is a handy tool for estimating wind speeds by observing the effect of wind on smoke and trees (see Table 2-1). A British admiral, Sir Francis Beaufort (1774–1857), designed the scale for ocean use, but it has been adapted for land observations. By using the Beaufort scale, a meteorologist like you can arrive at reasonable estimates of wind speed. For example, when you see smoke drifting, you will know that the wind speed is only a few miles per hour (mph). When you see small trees swaying, it means a fresh breeze is blowing at 19–24 mph (30–38 kilometers per hour, or kph).

Anemometer • *Anemometers* measure how fast the wind is blowing (Figure 2-1). They have between three and five cups to "catch" the wind. The faster the wind, the faster the cups spin. A meter on the instrument shows the wind speed.

To build an anemometer you will need the following materials:

- ballast (sand, birdseed, rice, cat litter)
- 2 old table-tennis balls
- small bud vase
- 3 wooden shishkebab skewers
- permanent felt-tip marking pen
- 13-oz coffee can
- Exacto knife
- 2½-inch-diameter Styrofoam ball

Place a bud vase in a coffee can. Fill the can two-thirds full with ballast to secure the bud vase in the can. Put one skewer all the way through the center of a Styrofoam ball. Be careful; the skewers are sharp. Carefully cut two old table-tennis balls in half using an Exacto knife. This will create four cups for catching the wind. Color one of the cups using a permanent marking pen.

Using another skewer, make a table-tennis-ball sandwich, with the Styrofoam ball in the middle. Repeat with the other skewer, aligning all skewers at 90-degree angles near the center of the Styrofoam ball. Place your anemometer into the bud vase with the point of the skewer facing down. Blow on your anemometer. Use a small fan or a hair dryer, too. What did you notice?

Figure 2–1. Clockwise from left:
homemade weather vane, rain gauge,
anemometer, and two mystery instruments.
(Build them yourself to find out
what they do; see pages 10, 14, 17.)

Were all the cups facing the same way? If not, align them and repeat the experiment. What did you notice? Place your anemometer outdoors in an open area. With a partner, make and record observations for a 30-second period. One partner should count the number of revolutions of the colored cup. The other should time the observation. The number of revolutions can be calibrated with the observed wind speed reported on radio or television and your observations of trees and smoke. In this way, you will create your own Beaufort-type wind scale. For example, suppose your instrument records 35 revolutions in a 30-second period and you observe leaves rustling and hear a television wind speed report of 6 mph (10 kph). Thirty-five revolutions fits a Beaufort category of 2. After using your instrument for several days, you should be able to add a column to the Beaufort scale which shows your instrument's revolution count.

Table 2-1. *Beaufort wind scale*

Beaufort Number	Speed kph	mph	Wind Name	Land indication
0	<1	<1	calm	Smoke rises vertically.
1	1–5	1–3	light air	Smoke drifts.
2	6–11	4–7	light breeze	Leaves rustle.
3	12–19	8–12	gentle breeze	Small twigs move.
4	20–29	13–18	moderate breeze	Small branches move.
5	30–38	19–24	fresh breeze	Small trees sway.
6	39–50	25–31	strong breeze	Large branches move.
7	51–61	32–38	moderate gale	Whole trees move.
8	62–74	39–46	fresh gale	Twigs break off trees.
9	75–86	47–54	strong gale	Branches break.
10	87–101	55–63	whole gale	Some trees uprooted.
11	102–119	64–73	storm	Widespread damage.
12	>120	≥74	hurricane	Severe destruction.

Wind Vane • *Wind vanes* tell the direction FROM WHICH the wind is blowing. The difference between the size of the arrowhead and tail ensures that the arrow points *into* the direction from which the wind comes. In New England, a wind from the east often brings cold, damp weather because the wind comes from the Atlantic Ocean. A west wind, blowing from the land, typically brings drier weather. In southern California, an east wind comes from the desert and is often hot and dry. West winds from the Pacific Ocean bring cool and wet weather. Wind vanes are sometimes decorated with animals and other shapes. These do not affect the way the vane works. What animals and shapes have you seen on wind vanes?

To make a wind vane (Figure 2-1) you will need the following:

- poster board (fluorescent colors)
- unsharpened pencils with erasers
- straight pin
- scissors
- stapler
- straw

Cut the arrowhead and tail out of the posterboard. Staple one arrowhead and one tail to the ends of a straw. Place a straight pin in the center of the straw and then push it partly into a pencil eraser. Hold the pencil in an upright position and test your vane with a small electric fan or hair dryer located a few feet away. Make several wind vanes, each with a different head and tail size, and evaluate their performance. Choose the one that seems to work the best. Which way does the arrow point?

Determine directions using a map of your area or a compass. On a day when the wind is blowing, hold the wind vane in an upright position outside. Compare and contrast your observation of wind direction with that reported on local television or radio weather reports.

13

Remember that your wind vane should point into the direction FROM WHICH the wind is blowing.

TEMPERATURE AND PRESSURE

Thermometer and Barometer • *Thermometers* measure *temperature*. The most common contain alcohol (colored red for easy viewing) or mercury in a glass tube. If you have a thermometer, touch the bulb at the bottom and watch what happens to the fluid. Assuming it's not a very hot summer day, your skin temperature should be warmer than the temperature of the air. As the temperature of the fluid increases, it expands (increases its volume) and the liquid "moves up" the tube. The opposite happens when temperatures fall. By knowing how much the fluid expands and contracts, thermometer makers are able to place appropriate temperature scales on the thermometer.

Another common thermometer is the bimetallic strip. You probably have one of these in the wall thermostat which controls the heating or air-conditioning system in your home. Carefully remove the cover of your thermostat and see if you can find a coiled metal strip. With adult permission, turn off the heating or cooling system. Use a hair dryer to blow hot air onto the thermostat. How does the coil strip change? There are actually two strips of metal joined together. Each strip has a different rate of expansion and contraction. As the temperature changes, the coil either enlarges or shrinks. Since the coil is attached to a pointer, you can read the temperature from a scale. After you have finished your observations, allow the thermostat to return to its original condition.

What other types of thermometers have you seen? How do you think these work?

Barometers measure air *pressure*, the weight of the air pushing down. Mercury barometers contain a tube

14

of mercury about 30 inches (76 cm) tall. They are expensive and complicated to use; they can be affected by changes in temperature, and are primarily used for *calibration* of aneroid barometers. The height of the mercury column, in "inches of mercury," is how pressure is reported during television or radio weather reports.

Aneroid barometers are "fluidless." They contain a vacuum canister and a pointer-gauge arrangement. As pressure changes, the barometer canister enlarges or shrinks slightly, but just enough for the pointer to move. Most home barometers are of this type.

The following instructions will guide you in building a barometer and a thermometer. We'll let you determine which is which through observations.

For one instrument you'll need:

- small, wide-mouthed glass jar (baby-food or vegetable)
- 14-inch or larger party balloon
- heavy-duty rubber band
- plastic coffee stirrer
- white school glue
- plastic ruler

Remove the neck of the balloon and make a cut from the edge of the balloon to its center. Stretch the balloon tightly over the mouth of the small jar. Wrap a rubber band around the bottle neck to hold the balloon in place. You may need some help in doing this.

Glue the end of a plastic coffee stirrer onto the center of the balloon. Allow to dry.

For the other instrument you'll need:

- plastic balloon stick or plastic straw
- cold glue gun or silicon caulking
- small glass soda-pop bottle with a metal screw-on cap
- plastic ruler
- blue food coloring

15

In the center of the metal cap carefully drill a hole large enough for a plastic balloon stick or straw to fit through. Don't make the hole too large! Fill the bottle about half full with water. Add a few drops of blue food coloring. Place the cap on the bottle and slide the plastic straw through the cap so that it extends into the colored water but does not rest on the bottom of the bottle. Mark the straw. Use a cold glue gun or silicon caulking to seal around the straw on both the inside and outside of the cap. Allow to dry.

Cap the bottle tightly. Blow air into the straw. Don't stop until the water level rises above the top of the bottle. Don't worry, the water will not come out of the straw!

Place both instruments in a part of your home away from air currents, heat, and light. Watch the instruments for several days and compare each with pressure and temperature observations given on television weather reports. Which instrument responds most to pressure changes? You've discovered the barometer!

Repeat this procedure, but use a hair dryer to heat both instruments. What do you notice? That's why the barometer must be kept in an inside location away from temperature changes. Place a ruler on top of the barometer or affix it to the wall behind the barometer to track movement of the fluid up and down the tube. Calibrate your barometer with observations given on radio, television, or telephone weather reports. If fluid sinks below the cap or stopper level, check for air leaks and reseal if necessary.

Place your thermometer in a shady outdoor location where it is protected from rain. Place a ruler next to the thermometer to track movement of the pointer.

For both of these instruments, the pointer or the fluid in the straw moves opposite to the way you think it should move. The pointer on the thermometer goes down as the temperature rises and the air inside the glass jar expands. As the outside air pressure increases it forces the fluid down the barometer tube.

PRECIPITATION

We left *precipitation* for last. What instruments do you think would be best for measuring rain and snow?

Rain Gauge • *Rain gauges* catch falling rain. A ruler or a scale on the rain gauge is used to measure how much rain fell. For reading rainfall more accurately, a smaller, calibrated gauge is often placed inside a larger one. This increases the depth of water in the gauge, allowing for easier reading.

To build a rain gauge (Figure 2-1), you'll need:

- plastic 2-liter soda bottle
- Exacto knife
- plastic ruler

Remove the label from the bottle and carefully cut off the tapered top using an Exacto knife. Fill the bottom of the bottle with about 1 inch (2.5 cm) of water to eliminate any irregularities in the shape of the bottle. This water will also weigh down the bottle in case it is windy outside. Place your rain gauge on a level surface, away from trees and building overhangs. Place a ruler next to the bottle and measure the depth of the water. This calibrates your rain gauge.

Invert and place the tapered top inside the gauge to act as a funnel for catching rainfall and a cover to reduce evaporation. Each day, even if it hasn't rained, read the gauge. If it has rained, subtract the previous reading from today's to determine how much rain fell. Whether or not it has rained, today's reading becomes the calibration for the next observation.

If excess evaporation occurs, refill the gauge with water. If too much rain falls, partially empty the gauge.

Always recalibrate your gauge whenever you add or remove water from it. Keep a record of the rainfall and compare it to what is reported in the newspaper and/or on television. Under what conditions are your observations closest to those of the official reports? Most different? One type of commercially made rain gauge is shown in Figure 2-2.

There are several ways to measure snowfall. Consider how snow collects on grassy areas and on concrete or asphalt surfaces. How does wind affect snow depth? Use a ruler or other measuring stick to determine how deep the snow is in several places. Be careful not to overestimate snowfall! If you measure in drifts, also measure in places where the wind has blown the snow away. Average your readings together to obtain a representative snowfall value.

Alternatively, measure snow as it falls on an exposed, nonwindblown or nondrifted, flat area. After measuring the snow, sweep the area clear of snow and let new snow accumulate. Several times during the snowstorm, measure snowfall and add the measurements together to obtain the total snowfall.

To measure the liquid water content of snow, empty your rain gauge or build a second one. Remove the funnel and invert the gauge over an area with representative snowfall. Press the gauge down into the snow. This gives you a *snow core* sample. Clear away the snow from the outside of the gauge. Slide a piece of cardboard under the gauge. Holding the cardboard in place, invert the gauge. Bring your snow core indoors and let it melt.

Pour the melted snow into another container. Fill the gauge with water and recalibrate it. Pour in the melted snow water and measure the change in water level. This is the "liquid equivalent" of the snowfall. Typically 10 inches (25 cm) of snow melts down to about 1 inch (2.5 cm) of water. The 10:1 ratio can be used to determine if snow is "wet" or "dry." Wet snow con-

Figure 2–2. A rain gauge on a fence post

tains more water (maybe 8 inches—20 cm—of snow will become 1 inch of water) and is sticky (great for building snowmen). Dry snow (maybe 12 inches—30 cm—of snow to produce 1 inch of water) is powdery and does not stick together well. When it snows, first estimate the water equivalent by determining how sticky the snow is. How accurate were your estimates?

Measure snow depth and take a snow core sample the day after it snows. How has the snow depth and the liquid equivalent relationship changed? Why do you think this occurred?

DATA COLLECTION

Now that you are armed with instruments, you are ready to collect and record weather data. Take a piece of lined paper and design a data sheet similar to the one shown in Figure 2-3. For at least two weeks, record weather conditions at the same time each day.

To round out your data collection, you can gather additional information from your local newspaper weather page, local telephone recording, television weather reports, or any professional weather instruments you may have. You'll learn how to measure dew point and determine relative humidity in Chapter 6. Cloud type and other sky observations will be described in Chapter 7. After collecting data, examine your observations carefully. Are there patterns? An easy way to find patterns is to graph your data.

You can create individual graphs or a "super graph" display, by pasting together graphs for several weather elements (Figure 2-4). As you compare your graphs, what relationships do you see? If you continue to collect and graph weather data for several months, seasonal and other weather relationships should emerge.

Are there any geographical features (such as lakes, oceans, or mountains) in your area which could affect

date	temp. °F	dew point °F	humidity %	pressure of mercury	Beaufort	direction/ speed	clouds	precipitation	remarks; other information
Mon Mar 4	53	42	62	29.80	4	SE 15	stratocumulus	– –	– –
Tue Mar 5	67	55	65	29.65	5	S 20	cumulus; cumulonimbus	– –	thunder and lightning to west
Wed Mar 6	42	30	62	29.98	5	NW 20	cumulus	0.45"	cold front passed 8 PM last night
Thu Mar 7	38	20	48	30.17	2	N 5	none; clear skies	– –	frost this morning
Fri Mar 8	47	24	40	30.15	3	S 10	cirrus	– –	blue sky; white cirrus streamers
Sat Mar 9	55	37	51	29.95	4	SW 15	altostratus; cumulus	– –	very windy this morning
Sun Mar 10	48	45	83	30.08	4	NW 15	cirrostratus; cumulus	0.02"	light rain showers around noon

Figure 2-3. *Sample data sheet for Raleigh, N.C., showing types of data that can be collected each day; 5 PM observation time.*

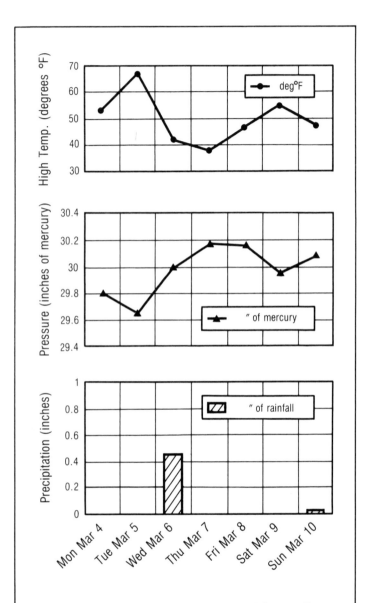

Figure 2-4. *Graphical representation of data in Figure 2-3 showing correlation of temperature, pressure, and precipitation during a seven-day period.*

your weather? Is there a preferred time for thunder-storms to occur? What about fog? Does the wind blow more from one direction? Using data from newspapers and television, compare your weather conditions with those in nearby cities. Are these cities affected by the same geographical features as your area? Is it warmer or colder in the mountains? near the coast? in the city? in the suburbs?

You can also learn about how the weather varies across a continent at about the same latitude. Select one of these city groupings: Portland (Oregon), Min-neapolis (Minnesota), Portland (Maine); San Francisco (California), Denver (Colorado), St. Louis (Missouri), Washington (DC); or Los Angeles (California), Dallas (Texas), Charleston (South Carolina). Use the news-paper weather page to collect data. Tabulate and graph observed high temperatures for your city group for a month. How does the temperature vary across the United States? Repeat this in another season. Does the temper-ature relationship change? If so, how? Why do you think this occurs?

WEATHER MAPPING

Weather maps are the meteorologist's way of making a picture of important weather data. Maps are often used to show both observed and forecast weather conditions at the ground and at various levels up to 10 miles (16 km) above sea level. We'll concentrate on ground-level weather maps at this time.

Figure 2-5 shows three *high-pressure systems* (H). Winds around each of these blow clockwise (in the di-rection the hands of a clock move) and outward. High-pressure systems usually represent *air masses*, large areas in which temperature and moisture values are similar. Highs generally bring "good" weather.

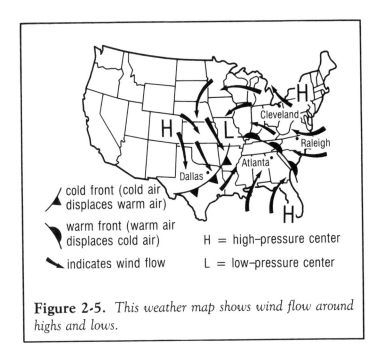

Figure 2-5. *This weather map shows wind flow around highs and lows.*

Between the highs are fronts and *low-pressure systems* (L). Just like fronts in wartime, weather fronts are the battlegrounds between air masses. In fact, this is how weather fronts earned their names. If the cold air pushes against the warm air and pushes it away, the front is a *cold front*. If the warm air wins the battle, it's a *warm front*. When neither air mass wins, the front doesn't move much and is called a *stationary front*. The barbs on the cold front and the half moons on the warm front point in the direction TOWARD WHICH the front is moving. Fronts and low-pressure centers are usually the places where rainy and stormy weather occur. Temperature, dew point, wind direction, pressure, and sky conditions often change abruptly along fronts.

On this map, winds near Dallas would be blowing from the northwest; at Cleveland from the southeast;

and at Atlanta from the southwest. As the storm system moves toward the northeast, winds at Atlanta will change direction. From which direction will the winds come once the cold front passes?

If you want to see how weather systems move, cut out the forecast newspaper weather maps for two consecutive days. Plot (using a colored pencil) the positions of highs, lows, and fronts from one map onto the other. What do you notice? Toward what direction do most weather features move across the United States? Why do you think this is so? Newspapers provide only forecast weather maps. To see how observed weather patterns move, watch television weather reports.

Now that you've seen how weather map features have moved, can you predict where they will be the next day? If you move the weather feature the same distance it moved from one day to the next, you can estimate where the feature will be a day later (see Figure 2-6).

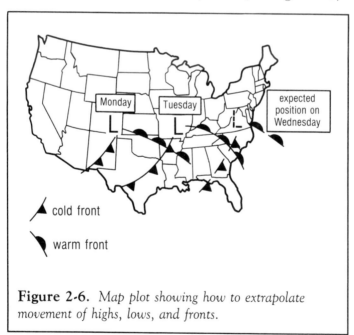

Figure 2-6. *Map plot showing how to extrapolate movement of highs, lows, and fronts.*

This is called *extrapolation*. Compare your prediction of where weather features will be with those of your television meteorologist. Compare both predictions to what actually happens. Pay special attention to your weather when a front is expected to pass your area. How do temperature, pressure, dew point, and wind change when the front goes by?

Follow the weather patterns and make your own weather map forecasts for a week or more. Extrapolation is only one way to predict future weather patterns, but it can be quite reliable under certain conditions.

Sun
and
Seasons

The Earth's movement around the sun and the tilt of the earth's axis creates our four seasons. We experience this throughout the year with seasonal temperature and weather changes and variations in the length of night and day. Some places don't have all four seasons. Others have a fairly uniform temperature throughout the year, but have rainy and dry seasons. These seasonal differences are what *climatologists* use to classify the *climate* of an area.

In addition to global, seasonal variations in temperature, there can be variations in your area because of geographical factors. But first you need to explore how heat transfer occurs in the atmosphere.

HEAT TRANSFER

Heat can be transferred from one object to another through three processes: radiation, conduction, and convection. Consider experiences you have had which involve heat transfer from one object or place to another. Do you know which process caused the transfer of heat?

Stand in a sunny location. Which side of your body gets warmer? Next, fill a coffee cup with hot water.

Carefully touch the outside of the cup. Place your hand slightly above the coffee cup. Can you feel the heat?

Energy from the sun travels through space and reaches Earth by *radiation*. You get warm while standing in the sun because you absorb this energy. The sun's energy is also absorbed by the Earth and this helps warm the Earth each day. But the Earth radiates energy back to space, both day and night. We don't notice this heat loss during the day. At night, especially when skies are clear, winds are light, and the air is relatively dry, heat loss can be dramatic. This radiation balance is a key factor in the heating and cooling process that causes seasons.

Conduction involves heat transfer by direct contact. When you touched the coffee cup, heat was transferred directly to your hand. Your hand "felt" hot. When the sun heats the ground through radiation, conduction is what transfers the heat from the ground to air that is in contact with the ground. At night, the air near the ground is cooled the same way.

Up and down motions in the atmosphere involve *convection*. Warm air is less dense than cold air and tends to rise, taking its heat with it. You felt this upward movement of warm air as you held your hand above the cup. Denser cold air tends to sink. You can verify this by opening the door of your refrigerator. Hold your hand above and below the open door. Where is it colder?

To simulate how convection appears in the atmosphere, you'll need two identical small, narrow-mouthed glass bottles, such as 10-ounce fruit juice bottles. Cut out a piece of poster board slightly larger than the mouths of the bottles. Fill one bottle with cold tap water; fill the other with warm tap water and add several drops of red food coloring. Put both bottles in the kitchen sink.

Place the piece of poster board on the mouth of the warm-water bottle and hold it there as you invert the bottle. Keeping the poster board in place, rest the inverted bottle on the other one so that the mouths of the two bottles are aligned. Now carefully remove the poster board. What do you observe? This type of layering, with warm air on top of cold, is what often happens at night. The Earth loses energy to space by radiation, and no sunlight is coming into the atmosphere to warm it. The air near the ground is cooled by direct contact with the colder ground. Atmospheric *stability* occurs when warm air lies on top of cold because the cold, dense air stays on the bottom.

What do you think will happen if you invert the bottle pair? This places warm water on the bottom and colder water on top. In the atmosphere, this is called *instability*.

There are many other opportunities to investigate heat transfer processes in and around your home. With adult supervision, turn on the oven in your kitchen to around 350°F (177°C). Once the oven has reached this temperature, carefully open the oven door and move away. Can you feel the heat radiating from the oven toward you?

Find a pencil and touch its eraser, its metal band, and its wooden part. Which part is coldest? Is it really colder than the other parts? Wasn't the entire pencil at room temperature? The reason why the metal felt colder was because metal is a good conductor of heat. When you touched the metal, heat was taken from your fingers and they felt colder.

Take a shower and get the bathroom really steamy. What do you notice about the steam? Step out from the shower and crouch down low. Is it colder or warmer closer to the floor?

Look around you and find other examples of heat transfer by radiation, conduction and convection. A good place to start is by helping to cook a spaghetti dinner. But think about how you make toast; how a fireplace warms a room; where heat escapes from a television set or VCR; and how snow melts on a roof.

Keep track of sunrise and sunset times for a week (Figure 3-1). The data is usually found on the newspaper weather page and given in television weather reports. You can also measure these times yourself. As you watch for sunrise or sunset, don't look directly at the sun; rather, just glance quickly in the direction of the sun to note when the sun first appears over the horizon (sunrise) or last appears (sunset).

How many hours and minutes of daylight do you experience each day? How does this change? Predict sunrise and sunset times and the length of day you would expect about one lunar cycle (thirty days) from now. What about sixty days? Ninety days? Remember to verify your predictions. If you would like to see a complete annual cycle covering all seasons, try graphing sunrise and sunset times once a week for a complete year. Keep your graph in a convenient place (for example, on the refrigerator door).

Make a sketch of your eastern horizon, carefully noting key objects such as water towers, tall buildings, trees, and mountains. Twice a month for several months, plot where the sun rises in relation to these fixed objects. Also, keep track of whether the sun is high or low in the sky at noon. For each observation, record the high and low temperatures that day. Relate where the sun rises, its midday position in the sky, the length of daylight, and the temperatures you observe. What can you conclude?

Shine a flashlight on a wall to simulate sunlight striking the earth's surface. When the flashlight is aimed directly at the wall this simulates the sun high in the sky at midday. The sun's rays strike the Earth more directly and are very concentrated. Now move the flashlight so it shines on the wall at a 45-degree angle. This simulates a sun low in the sky with its rays more dis-

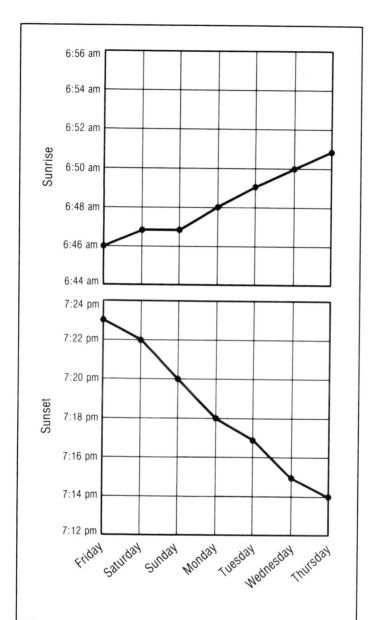

Figure 3-1. *Graph plots of sunrise and sunset over a seven-day period.*

persed. Under which condition do you think temperatures on Earth would be warmest?

Seasonal weather changes are primarily driven by differences in the angle at which the sun's rays strike the Earth and the length of daylight. Other factors influence seasons, too. There are differences in how the sun's rays heat different land surfaces. There are also differences between how the sun's rays heat land and water.

LAND DIFFERENCES

On a sunny day, fill four storage bags half full with cold tap water and seal them tightly. Place three of the bags in sunny places: one on a blacktop surface or a piece of black construction paper, another on a grassy area, and the third on a piece of white paper. Place the fourth bag in any shady location (such as the shadow of a building or under a tree). These represent only four of many possible land surfaces. Return an hour later. Touch each bag or measure the water temperature using a thermometer. Which bag was hottest? coldest? Think about why. Repeat the experiment in a different season and compare your observations.

Check your wardrobe for seasonal colors. When do you tend to wear dark-colored clothes—during the summer or winter? On a warm, sunny day, wear a white shirt and dark pants. Stand outside for a few minutes with your back to the sun. Which gets hotter, your top or your bottom? Explore your neighborhood and catalog the different land colors that are present. How does this change from one part of the year to another?

Dark objects tend to absorb sunlight. Light-colored objects reflect it. Thus, some land areas on Earth will become warmer than others just because of their color.

Go outside on a cold morning before the sun rises and touch several different objects (for example, a car, a car tire, a leaf, a tree trunk, the ground, the side of your home). Measure the temperature of these also. (To measure the temperature of a leaf, carefully lay the thermometer on it, or on a branch so that the bulb of the thermometer is touching the leaf.) Which objects are coldest? Keep a list. How do your observations compare with the results of the pencil experiment?

What happens to the temperatures of objects on a hot afternoon? Carefully touch the same objects. Which were hottest? Make another list. Compare lists of hottest and coldest objects. Is there any relationship?

Since conduction transfers heat through direct contact, air next to cold objects becomes cold and air next to warmer objects becomes warmer. This is how the daily temperature cycle works.

LAND AND WATER DIFFERENCES

Fill one glass jar with water and another with soil. Shine a flashlight through each to simulate sunlight striking earth and water. Light passes through the water more easily. That's why you can see underwater but need artificial light to see in a cave.

Find a soil (or sand) area near where you live. Touch it on a sunny afternoon. The soil should feel warm. Dig down several inches and touch the soil in the hole. How does it feel? What can you say about heat transfer in the soil? Remember to put the soil back in the hole.

Fill a pail with cool water. Place it in a sunny location and let it sit for several hours. Touch the surface of the water and then place your hand into the pail. Did you notice any difference in temperature?

Because water is transparent, sunlight can pass into it and heat it through a greater depth. Soil is not transparent and absorbs the sun's rays only at its surface.

Partially fill a bathtub with warm water. Then add

cold water without stirring. Do the cold and warm water mix? Test the water at each end of the bathtub to verify. What happens if you move the water around with your hand? In bodies of water, currents and waves help to mix the water in much the same way. How is this temperature transfer different from what occurs in soil? Generally soil doesn't move. The only way that heat is transferred is by conduction. During the day, heat is usually transferred slowly down into the soil; at night, heat is usually transferred upward.

LOCAL EFFECTS

On a sunny day during the warmer months of the year, the land will become warmer than a nearby water body (such as a lake, bay, ocean). Due to conduction, the air over land will also be warmer than air over the water. If you live near the water, you may have gone there just to cool off. Often, cool winds will blow from the water during the day, creating a "sea breeze" (Figure 3-2).

The land also loses its heat faster than water. At night, areas near the water will often be warmer than areas just a few miles inland. Winds may now blow from land to water, creating a "land breeze."

SEASONAL EFFECTS

By experiencing the daily heating and cooling cycle of land and water, you have simulated the larger-scale seasonal effect. During the warmer months of the year, land areas are continually warmed faster than nearby water areas. So by late summer, the land-water temperature difference is usually the greatest. The cooling effect that happens during the fall and winter months usually results in the land becoming colder than the nearby water.

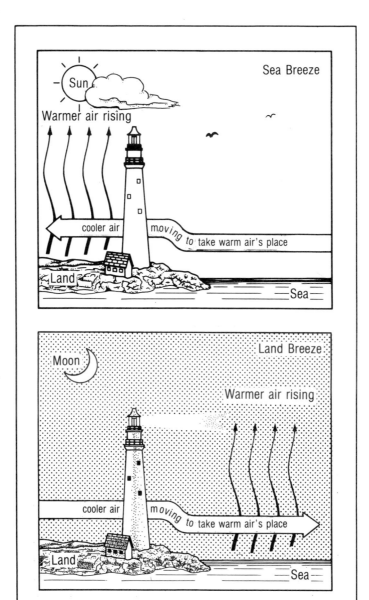

Figure 3-2. *Why sea breezes tend to occur during the day, while land breezes occur in the evening.*

You can see this effect by graphing the daily temperatures in a coastal city versus a nearby inland city for a week. Information on daily high and low temperatures is readily available on your newspaper weather page and on television weather reports. Collect and record data each day and compute a daily temperature range for each city.

Repeat the data collection project during another season. Did the daily temperature range for coastal and inland cities differ between seasons? During which season was the high temperature warmest over inland areas? The low temperature? Note that passage of storm systems and weather fronts can disrupt the expected temperature pattern.

Pressure
and
Wind

Every television, radio, and telephone weather report includes a barometer reading. Do you know what this means? In earlier times, sailors and others believed that high pressure meant "good" weather and low pressure "bad." Is this always true?

Observe how atmospheric pressure changes for several weeks. Read your barometer and/or obtain barometer data from television, radio, or telephone weather reports. Record barometer readings and daily weather conditions. What relationship do you notice between them? Between pressure changes and weather? Which help you to better predict the upcoming weather: pressure or pressure change?

Let's begin by verifying that air exists and that there is atmospheric pressure. Take an empty glass and stuff a dry paper towel into it. Invert the glass into a bowl of water so that it is at least halfway submerged. Remove the glass, without tilting it. Remove the paper towel. Is it wet or dry? Explain.

Repeat the experiment. As you remove the glass, tilt it. What do you observe? Was the glass really empty? Why didn't the water come up into the glass during the first experiment?

Place a straw into a glass of water. Remove the straw. Nothing stays in the straw. Repeat, but this time place your finger tightly over the top of the straw before you lift the straw out of the water. Then release your finger. What comes out of the straw? What was the difference between these two experiments?

Repeat the experiment one more time. Before releasing your finger from the top of the straw, place a finger from your other hand on the bottom of the straw. After releasing the first finger, turn the straw upside down. Does the water stay in the straw? Can you explain what is happening?

All of these experiments have shown that air pressure exists. And air pressure is caused because air has *weight* or *mass*. Suppose we could capture a vertical column of air from the bottom to the top of the atmosphere. Let's allow this column to have an area of 1 square inch at the bottom. The atmosphere in this column would weigh 14.7 pounds (6.7 kg). As a result, the atmosphere in this column would be pushing down with a force of 14.7 pounds per square inch. This is the average sea-level pressure on the Earth.

Atmospheric pressure pushes downward and affects everything on the Earth, including your body. You would be crushed by this force if your body did not have its own internal forces which push outward. One body force that you may be familiar with is blood pressure. Have a school nurse measure your blood pressure. Interview the nurse about what blood pressure is and what it means to your health. Discuss this with other members of your family.

Have you ever heard the expression, "walking on air"? Is this possible? Examine the tires on your bicycle or the family car. Each tire has information that describes its proper inflation pressure. Every tire must be inflated to a pressure greater than 14.7 pounds per square inch to compensate for the pressure of air outside the tire. Because bicycle tires have smaller volumes and smaller surface areas than automobile tires, they have to be inflated to higher pressures. The difference between the pressure inside a tire and the atmospheric pressure outside is what allows a tire to stay round even when holding up a car or a bicycle. You can also inflate an air mattress and walk on it. Many carnivals have special attractions which involve "walking or bouncing on air." In all of these situations, there is air between you and the ground.

Can you discover other ways that pressure is used around your home? Can you tell how these work?

Almost fill a 1- or 2-liter plastic soda bottle. Insert a glass medicine dropper into the bottle, squeezing the cap to partially fill the dropper with water. Let the dropper fall into the bottle and cap the bottle. Gently squeeze the bottle. What happens to the medicine dropper? Can you suspend the dropper in the middle of the bottle? If you can't find a glass medicine dropper, try weighting a plastic one with small nails.

Gently squeeze an unopened bag of pretzels or potato chips. There is air inside. Why do you think it is there? What happens when you open the bag? Does air rush in or out? How does this pressure help to seal the bag and keep the food fresher? What about a jar of pickles? a can of vegetables? If your family uses plastic food storage containers, what must be done to reduce the air pressure inside the container in order to seal it?

Fill a plastic 2-liter soda bottle half full of very warm tap water. Cap the bottle quickly and allow it to stand for a moment or two. Open the bottle and pour out the water and then quickly recap the bottle. Predict what will happen in a few minutes. Was your prediction correct?

Refill the bottle with cool tap water and cap the bottle. While the bottle is in your kitchen sink, carefully stick two pushpins into one side of the bottle, both below the water level. One pin should be about an inch (2.5 cm) below the water line; the other an inch below the first pin. What do you think will happen if you remove the top pin? the bottom pin? both pins? Repeat the experiment after you partially unscrew the cap. What did you observe that was different?

There was more pressure on the bottom hole than the top one because there was more weight of water above it. The same holds true in the atmosphere. Pressure is greatest near the ground and less the higher up you go. An experiment performed in France in the mid-1600s demonstrated this. By carrying a barometer up a tall mountain, it was shown that pressure got lower the higher one climbed. What effect might this have on people who live in mountain areas? on pilots who fly aircraft at very high altitudes? or on athletes who compete in places like Denver, the "mile-high city"?

WIND

Wind usually occurs because pressure differs from place to place. Stand face-to-face with a partner. Press your hands against those of the other person. Both partners should now push hard. Whoever has the greater force or pressure pushes the other away. In the atmosphere, there is a similar push away from high to low pressure. The greater the difference in pressure between highs and lows, the greater the resulting wind. The pressure difference between the inside and outside of hurricanes and tornadoes is very great!

Observe and measure wind speed and direction. What do you notice? Under what conditions does the wind blow fastest? From which direction does the wind blow the strongest? From which direction does the wind blow most often?

Meteorologists name winds FROM WHERE THEY COME. This is because winds bring certain conditions with them. A north wind blows from the north and usually brings colder weather. An east wind blows from the east. Along the New England and Middle Atlantic coasts of the United States, an east wind brings cooler, more humid weather; an east wind in California often brings hot, dry weather. A sea breeze blows from the sea. From what direction does the wind blow most often when it rains or snows?

The Earth's rotation produces another force, called the *Coriolis Force*, which deflects the air to the right in the Northern Hemisphere and to the left in the Southern Hemisphere. As the air moves, *friction* slows it down. Friction is a force that slows down any moving thing. Some surfaces create a greater frictional force than others. Roll a ball across a rug and then across a bare floor. Do you think friction is greater (and wind speed less) over tree-covered land or over prairies? As a result of pressure and Coriolis and frictional forces, air spirals OUT FROM high-pressure systems and INTO low-pressure systems.

Without small-scale variations in wind due to buildings, mountains, and other obstacles, you can locate the center of highs and lows quite easily (Figure 4-1). With the wind to your back, turn about 30 degrees to your right. The high-pressure center is to your right and the low-pressure center to your left. This relationship, known as Buys Ballot's law, was discovered by Christoph Buys Ballot, a Dutch meteorologist who lived in the 1800s. Using his law, compare your estimate of where the pressure systems are to what is shown on television weather reports. You can also relate expected winds to forecast positions of highs and lows. If, for example, the wind is blowing from the northeast, then stand with your back to the northeast. Turn slightly to your right. High pressure would be to your north (or right) and low pressure would be to your south (or left). Along the east coast, this would be a rainy or snowy weather pattern.

Wind speed and direction can vary significantly from

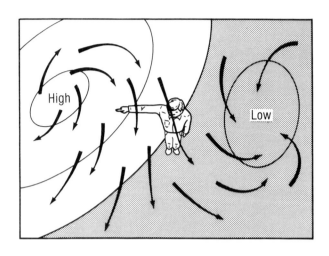

Figure 4-1. *How to locate high and low pressure centers. Stand with the wind at your back, and turn about 30 degrees to your right. The high pressure center will be to your right and the low pressure center to your left.*

one place to another. Part of this is tied to friction. Part is tied to how the wind blows around and over obstacles like mountains and buildings.

Carefully place a candle in a small candlestick holder behind an obstacle (for example, a can or a box). Light the candle. Place your face at the same level as the candle and the obstacle, checking to be sure the candle flame is completely hidden from your view. Blow hard toward the obstacle. Were you able to blow out the candle? How did you do it? Repeat this using obstacles that are shaped differently. Which shape is easier for the wind to blow around? How does this relate to the shapes of things that move in the atmosphere (birds, hot-air balloons, planes, cars, rockets, etc.). Why are these objects *aerodynamically* designed?

Imagine the wind blowing around a building. The

building deflects the wind and allows it to appear behind the obstacle just as it did in the above experiment. If there are several obstacles near each other, winds will often funnel quickly around these. In cities, this creates a wind tunnel effect. In mountain areas, high winds often blow quickly through passes or gaps. Some well-known mountain winds are the Chinook (west winds that blow down the eastern slopes of the Rocky Mountains) and the Santa Ana (east winds that blow downhill across southern California).

Be on the lookout for the effects of wind. You've already used the Beaufort wind scale (Chapter 2) to estimate the wind's effect on trees. You can also watch how leaves, snow, sand, and water react to the wind. How do you think snowdrifts and sand dunes are formed? If the wind does not cooperate, create your own drifts or dunes using a leaf blower or a fan.

As drifts and dunes are created in one place, sand, soil, leaves, or snow has to be removed from someplace else (Figure 4-2). Thus, wind both builds up and tears down. Wind can sometimes pick up large amounts of sand or soil and create sand or dust storms, as well as remove topsoil. These storms can reduce visibility, making driving hazardous. Some of the worst dust storms in United States history occurred during the 1930s. A lack of rainfall, poor crop-growing practices, and strong winds created a "Dust Bowl" across a large part of the central United States.

Take a piece of sandpaper and rub it on a piece of scrap wood. What happens to the wood? What happens if you rub faster? harder? What happens if you use different grades of sandpaper? What do you think would happen to a car caught in a sandstorm? What would happen to rocks or boulders?

You can experience the force of the wind in many ways (for example, riding your bicycle, skating, running, or walking). How hard do you have to work when

Figure 4–2. What are the factors that determine the shape of sand dunes?

moving with the wind as compared to when you move against it? What effect do you think wind has on airplanes? The United States lies primarily in the zone of prevailing westerly winds. Using an airline flight schedule, compare the length of time for east-to-west and west-to-east nonstop flights between the same cities. Which flight should take longer? Why do you think so? Be sure to adjust your computations for time zone changes.

Temperature

Temperature is a measure of the relative warmth or coldness of everything. The sun is hot (over 10,000°F, or 5500°C); the Earth is not (−60°F to +120°F, or −51°C to +49°C). Dry ice (frozen carbon dioxide) is about −109°F (−78°C). How hot do you think lightning is? At what temperature must food be kept in your refrigerator to prevent spoiling? At what temperature will ice melt? Will water freeze? At what temperature must you cook certain foods to ensure that bacteria are killed? All of these questions and more show just how dependent we are upon knowledge of temperature information.

THERMOMETERS

Do you consider yourself a good thermometer? Check yourself out. Fill three bowls with water. The left bowl should contain very warm tap water; the middle, room-temperature water; and the right, very cold tap water. Place your left hand in the bowl with warm water and your right hand in the bowl with cold water. After about a minute, place both hands in the middle bowl. How do your hands feel?

Think about how you, your family members, and your friends experience different temperatures. Do you always feel warm and toasty or are you chilly sometimes? Is everyone in the family always content with the heating or air-conditioning level? Do all your friends wear the same amount of clothing each day? These all indicate that we, as humans, are very poor thermometers.

How does your dog, cat, hamster, bird, or other nonwater pet feel to your touch? Do you have a reptile for a pet? If not, visit a nature center, zoo, or pet store, and ask for permission to touch a reptile's skin. Does it feel warm or cold? Touch different objects in your home. Which feel coldest? What is common about these? Insert a metal spoon and a wooden spoon into a bowl of very warm water. Which one gets hottest? If you live in a snowy area, make a snowball. Why do your hands get colder? Why does the snow stick together?

All of these show that heat is transferred from one object to another by contact. This is called conduction. Thermometers measure temperature by conduction, too. To use a thermometer, we place the bulb next to or into what we want to measure.

Since you now have an idea of which materials transfer heat most quickly (that is, the good *conductors*), you should be able to find materials around your home that are poor heat conductors (that is, the good *insulators*). Find some insulators and show how these help to keep warm objects warm or cold objects cold.

On a warm day, place three 12-ounce (340-g) cans of chilled soda outdoors in the shade. Wrap one in a kitchen towel; place another in an insulated ice chest or can holder; do nothing to the third. Return in about 3 hours. Compare the temperatures of the three cans using a thermometer or by a touch comparison. What can you conclude about insulation?

Cover yourself with a blanket or towel. Do you feel warmer or colder than you did before you covered yourself? Add a second blanket or towel. How do you feel now? Now put your head under the blanket. Do you feel warmer or colder? Why do you think people wear hats?

Visit a hardware store or lumberyard and examine the various household insulation products for sale. Interview a salesperson to learn about what these have in common and how they work. Contact your local power company for additional information.

Which of your clothes makes you feel the warmest? Which keeps you coolest? Compare characteristics of your clothes with those of household insulation.

It's possible to change the temperature of an object without adding or removing heat. This can be done by chemical reactions. Sprinkle salt on one end of an ice cube. What do you think will happen? Why? Examine the ice cube closely. In what other ways have you seen salt mixed with ice or snow?

Fill a medium-sized bowl about a quarter full with ice. Add a layer of salt. Then add alternate layers of ice and salt until the layering reaches almost to the top. Stir the mixture using a wooden spoon. Watch the outside of the bowl. What do you observe? Measure the temperature of the mixture at one-minute intervals throughout this experiment. At what temperature does frost form? How cold does the ice-salt mixture get? How can you lower the temperature further? Try this experiment using ice chips or snow and different types of salt. How do your results compare?

Be very careful when you do this experiment. The mixture is cold enough to cause frostbite if you accidentally touch the bowl or the ice-salt mixture. **Wear gloves!** Place your mixture in a safe place and let it melt. Pour through a strainer to collect any salt. Dispose of the salt in your normal household trash. Pour the water down the drain, diluting it with running tap water.

Take your thermometer (home-built or purchased)

outside during the middle of a sunny day. Measure the temperature over several different surfaces at several heights above ground. You can use your body to keep the thermometer shaded. Be careful how you hold your thermometer so you don't measure the temperature of your hands. What do you notice? Where is it hottest? coolest? Repeat this experiment early in the morning (especially during cooler months of the year). What do you notice?

During the day, the temperature is usually warmest near the ground. At night, the reverse occurs. Which of the heat transfer processes do you think is at work?

Next place your thermometer on the ground in direct sunlight. How hot or cold does it get? Have you seen sporting events in which a large thermometer is placed on the ground in a similar manner and the temperature is reported as 120°F (49°C) or more? The reported temperature is actually that of a heated thermometer and the temperature of the surface the thermometer is lying on. It is not the temperature of the air.

Because the temperatures can be very different over different surfaces, meteorologists from around the world have agreed to take consistent readings from inside a white louvered building (white to reflect sunlight; louvered to ensure ventilation) at a height of 4 to 5 feet (1.2–1.5 m) above the ground in a grassy area (Figure 5-1 and 5-2).

Where does your television meteorologist take his or her temperature readings? How about those displayed on a bank sign? Find out where the thermometer is located and how this may affect the reliability of the observation.

Take an early morning drive with an adult family member. Stop and measure the temperature at various places along a 3- to 5-mile (5–8 km) route. How does

Figure 5–1. To ensure consistency
in temperature readings from different
climates around the world, meteorologists
use instrument shelters like this one.
They are white, louvered, boxlike
structures at a height of 4 to
5 feet above the ground and
located in a grassy area.

Figure 5–2. Can you explain why snow covers only part of this roof?

the temperature change? If you go up and down hills, measure the temperature at crests and valleys. Repeat the experiment in the afternoon. What similarities or differences do you notice between the two data sets?

TEMPERATURE GRAPHING

From television or newspaper weather reports, compare observed high and low temperatures for several locations in and near your town or at a nearby city. For which location is the low temperature consistently lower? Is the high temperature consistently higher? Make a line graph of daily low temperatures for a month using a different color for each observation location. Do the same for high temperatures. What do you notice?

Measure or record changes in air temperature (and other weather elements) throughout a full day for several days (Figure 5-3). Use the time-record feature on your VCR to obtain values from The Weather Channel after you go to sleep. How does the temperature change during the morning? evening? when clouds cover the sun? when a thunderstorm passes? Graph your data.

Make a temperature scroll for your area for a complete year. Tape together, on the back side of graph paper, as many sheets as necessary. Get normal (or average) daily high and low temperatures, as well as observed highs and lows. Using a different color for each temperature type, make a four-line graph. What do you notice about the normal temperature variation from day to day? How about the actual temperatures?

Look for places where the observed high temperatures are more than the corresponding normal high temperatures. Shade the area between the observed and normal temperatures in red. Repeat for observed low temperatures that are warmer than normal. These indicate times when above-normal readings were observed. Do the same for both high and low temperatures that

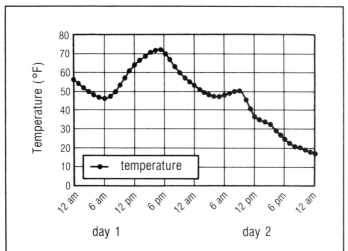

Figure 5-3. *An hourly temperature graph for Denver, Colorado. Notice that the expected daily temperature cycle was interrupted at about 8 AM on the second day. What weather event do you think could have caused this?*

are below normal. Shade these areas blue. You'll find many alternating places where red areas lie above normal lines and blues lie below. What type of patterns do you see?

Average each month's daily high and low temperatures to obtain an average monthly temperature. Make a line graph of this. Add average monthly precipitation as a column graph at the bottom. A sample is shown in Figure 5-4. This is called a *climograph* and is an easy way to represent the temperature and rainfall patterns which define the climate of a place. Find monthly temperature and rainfall data for other places around the world. Make climographs of these. How are they similar? different? How does your climograph compare with that of a city at the same latitude but hundreds of miles away?

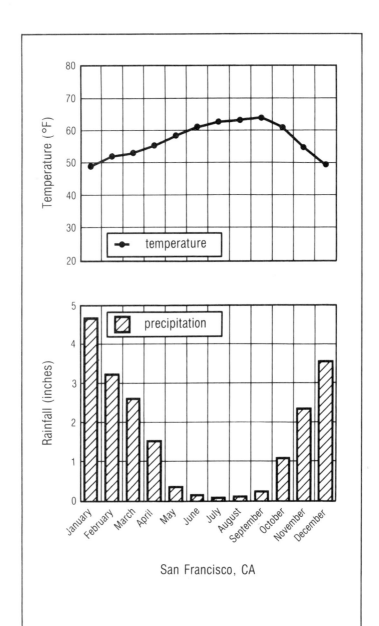

Figure 5-4. *Climograph for San Francisco, California.*

ISOTHERM ANALYSIS

In Chapter 2 you compared daily temperature readings at different cities along the same latitude. Another way to compare cities is to do an *isotherm* analysis of a weather map (Figure 5-5). An isotherm is a line along which all temperature values are the same. It's very much like a contour or elevation map that geologists use to describe the shape and slope of the land.

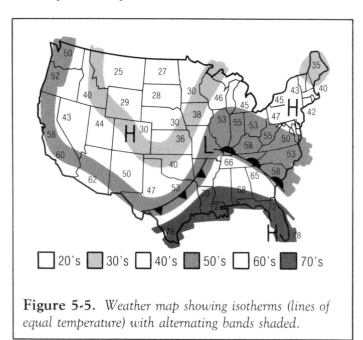

Figure 5-5. *Weather map showing isotherms (lines of equal temperature) with alternating bands shaded.*

Trace the outline of the United States and the contiguous forty-eight states from your newspaper weather page, atlas, or other source. The map should fill most of a 8½-by-11-inch page. Make extra copies so you'll have them handy. Plot the forecast high temperature for today for the United States cities listed in your newspaper weather-page tables. If necessary, use an atlas to locate cities. If too many cities are located in a small area, choose only one of the cities. Then use colored pencils and lightly shade or mark all cities whose temperatures will be in the 60s. Using a different color or marking pattern, shade the cities with highs in the 50s. Repeat until all temperatures are accounted for. Then draw black lines to separate the color bands. These lines represent temperatures at 10° increments (e.g., 40°, 50°, 60°). Compare your final map with that shown on the newspaper weather page. Is yours similar?

Although these temperatures are the ones expected at the ground, the shape of the isotherm pattern gives very important information about the wind pattern in the upper levels of the atmosphere (around 30,000 to 40,000 feet, or 9,000 to 12,000 m). Imagine you are standing on an isotherm, with cold temperatures to your left and warm temperatures to your right. The upper winds would be blowing into your back and moving away from you in the direction toward which you are looking. In the map shown in Figure 5-4, the wind at Kansas City would be blowing from the northwest and the wind at Washington, D.C. would be from the southwest. What would the upper-level winds be at Detroit, Michigan? This technique DOES NOT work well west of the Continental Divide because mountains and other local factors affect temperature patterns too much.

Where the isotherms are closer together, upper-level winds are usually blowing faster. And where the isotherms are closest together is usually where the *jet stream* is found. The jet stream is the location of the highest speed winds. Sometimes there will be more than one jet stream on your weather map.

The upper winds often carry ground-level weather systems (highs, lows, and fronts) with them. Knowledge of upper winds can help you forecast the direction in which these systems should move. You don't know wind speed values, so you can only estimate how fast the weather systems will move.

To verify the upper-level wind direction, watch high-altitude cirrus clouds move past a fixed ground-based object (for example, a telephone pole or roof). The direction of movement should be close to that expected from the isotherm pattern.

Moisture

Figure 6-1 shows a U.S. weather map with clouds and precipitation. Water in the atmosphere takes on many forms. The amount of water in the air varies greatly from place to place throughout the day. *Dew* can form and evaporate in a few hours; dark clouds and blue sky can be seen together; it can rain in some parts of town and not in others.

WATER CYCLE

Take a moment to think about all the places you have seen water in the atmosphere and on the ground. Where does the water go after a rain? How do clouds form and precipitate? These questions and others provide a framework for understanding the *water cycle*.

The water cycle describes how water changes its form and moves about the globe. In some local areas (such as deserts), the water cycle is out of balance. Without irrigation or other human intervention, plant and animal life could not exist. In some places, too much *precipitation* causes flooding.

You've seen water in many places, including rivers, lakes, streams, oceans, and even small puddles. Water from these, and water given off by plants and animals, evaporates into the air, changing into an invisible gas

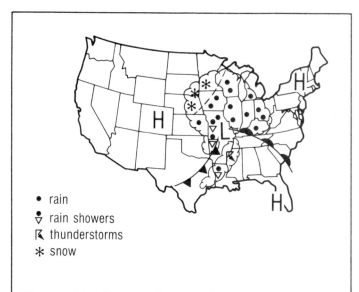

• rain
⊻ rain showers
Ⓡ thunderstorms
✳ snow

Figure 6-1. *This weather map shows precipitation associated with a low-pressure system.*

called *water vapor.* As the air becomes saturated, the water vapor condenses (changes from vapor to liquid) and clouds form. When air is *saturated,* it is holding all of the water vapor it can. At most, this may account for about 4% of the weight of the air. Eventually, the clouds may rain, snow, hail, or sleet. As precipitation falls to the ground, it runs off, filling lakes, rivers, and ponds. This latter stage of the water cycle is called *accumulation.* The cycle repeats itself. Plants and animals have their own water cycles. Can you describe these?

You can experience many parts of the water cycle in your own shower. This works best during the colder months of the year. Close the door to the bathroom and turn on the shower so that the water is warm to your touch. The air will quickly become more moist and a cloud will soon form. *Condensation* occurred because of two factors: (1) water vapor was added to the air, and (2) the air warmed by the steamy shower was cooled by conduction as it came in contact with the cooler air in the bathroom. These are two of the three ingredients needed for clouds to form. We'll discuss the third ingredient in the next chapter.

A terrarium is another ideal place to see the water cycle. In a large glass bowl or fish tank, build a miniature garden. Use small leafy plants and potting soil. Water the garden and then cover it with a piece of plastic wrap. Place the terrarium near a sunny window. In a few days, look at the terrarium. What do you notice? As long as it is covered, do you think the terrarium will ever run out of water?

EVAPORATION AND CONDENSATION

Evaporation occurs when water becomes water vapor. Fill a small flat dish with water and leave it in a sunny place. What happens? Step out of a swimming pool. How do you dry off without using a towel?

Place a mirror by your mouth and breathe on it. Even in warm weather, your moist breath will form fog on the mirror (this is condensation). Watch what happens to the fog. On a cold, rainy day, go outside and breathe heavily. Can you see your breath? How long does it last before it evaporates? What do you think you will see on a cold, dry day?

While dinner is being prepared, visit your kitchen. What is the steam that comes from the pot of boiling water or from the bowl of cooked vegetables? To see evaporation in plants (called *transpiration*), tie a plastic sandwich bag onto a leaf or cluster of leaves. Be sure the bag is tightly sealed. Predict what you think you will see in a few days.

Thoroughly wet three paper towels. Lay one flat in a shady place. Place the other two (one crumpled and one flat) in a sunny location. Predict which one will dry first. What are some other weather factors that aid evaporation and drying?

Once water vapor gets into the air, condensation is the next step in making precipitation. The small droplets you see when condensation first occurs are similar to small cloud or drizzle droplets.

On a warm day, place a glass of ice water onto a tray. Come back an hour later. You'll likely find that the tray will contain a puddle of water and that the glass will be wet. Where did the water come from?

Water vapor in the air condensed and appeared on the glass. It did this because the air next to the cold glass was cooled to its *dew point temperature* by conduction. Cold air cannot hold as much water as warm air. We'll discuss dew point in more detail later in this chapter.

PRECIPITATION

Using a plant mister, spray water onto a piece of wax paper. You'll notice many small droplets. Move a small droplet with a toothpick so that it touches one of its neighbors. What happens? Repeat this several times. The process by which raindrops grow by colliding with or capturing other drops is called *coalescence* or *accretion*, respectively.

Fill two small plastic margarine containers about three-quarters full with tap water. One should contain hot water, the other warm. Place covers loosely over the containers and put them in your refrigerator for several hours. Carefully remove the lids without disturbing the water droplets (this may take some practice). What do you notice? Where did the water droplets come from? Why are the droplets bigger in one container than the other? Hold the lids vertically. Do the droplets move? Tap the lids. What happens to the droplets? How can this movement occur in the atmosphere?

When you take a shower, watch the water droplets on the shower wall, door or curtain. When it rains, watch the droplets on a car window when the car is standing still and again when the car is in motion. What's the difference?

With adult supervision, boil a pot of water on the stove. Fill a frying pan with ice. Using a pot holder, hold the pan several inches above the pot of boiling water. What do you see on the bottom of the pan? After several minutes what happens? Move the pan away from the boiling water and carefully touch its bottom. Is it hot or cold? Can you explain why?

Can you tell the difference between a heavy rain shower and drizzle? Because raindrops splatter when they hit the ground or water, it is very difficult to measure them to determine their sizes. It's easier to measure snowflakes. You can catch flakes on a dark object (for example, a car, a ski jacket, or black construction paper) and use a magnifying glass to see their size and shape. Be careful not to breathe on them! What do you notice about the flakes?

You can capture raindrops and preserve them. Do this experiment on a normal rainy or drizzly day—but, for safety reasons, not during a thunderstorm! Sift a thin layer of cornstarch onto a cookie sheet or an oven pan. This will act as your raindrop collector. Place the pan outdoors for 5 seconds away from trees or building overhangs. Then bring the pan inside and pour the cornstarch through a fine mesh strainer. Most of the starch will pass through the strainer. What's left will be a collection of "fossilized" raindrops. These will be larger than the original raindrops. Do you know why?

Sort and count the drops by size and record the distribution and the type of rain event. Save your raindrops in carefully marked and sealed plastic bags. Repeat the process on other rainy days, using the same materials. The only variable that changes is the type of rain event. Is there a relationship between the size and the number of drops? The type of event and the number of drops? And how much rain actually fell and the size of the drops?

Compute the area of your raindrop collector. How many raindrops fell per square inch per minute? per hour? Approximately how many raindrops do you think might fall if this amount of rain were to fall on a baseball or soccer field? What about your town or city?

ACCUMULATION

When precipitation reaches the ground, most of it runs downhill into storm drainage systems, creeks, streams, and rivers. Eventually the water reaches lakes, reservoirs, and oceans. Some rainwater seeps into the ground, where it is absorbed by plants. All of these account for rainfall accumulation.

After a rain, watch how water moves toward lower elevations. As water runs off lawns, driveways, and sidewalks into the street, notice how small streams merge. If you live near converging rivers, observe the flow.

When snow melts, it produces small streams of water. In the mountains, these can merge to create rapidly flowing rivers. In flatter locations, these snowmelt streams make meandering paths in and under the snow and ice.

Which of the following result in faster or increased runoff—Bare soil, grassy soil, sand, land with trees, flat terrain, steep terrain, concrete, asphalt, frozen ground, ground saturated with water from previous rains?

DEW POINT AND RELATIVE HUMIDITY

The dew point is the temperature at which dew, or condensation, forms during cooling. It is the most direct and useful measure of atmospheric moisture. Look outside at various times during the day. When do you observe dew on leaves, grass, and cars? Why do you think it's generally found at these times? In cold weather, water vapor may change directly to *frost*. This is called *deposition*. When frost or snow changes directly to water vapor it is called *sublimation*.

The dew point tells us several things about the water content of the atmosphere. It tells the temperature at which condensation will occur. It also tells us how much water vapor is ACTUALLY in the air. Temperature, on the other hand, tells us how much vapor the air COULD hold.

Figure 6-2 shows that air with a dew point temperature of 70°F (21°C) ACTUALLY HOLDS slightly more than six times as much water vapor as air with a dew point temperature of 20°F (−7°C). Air with a temperature of 80°F (27°C) COULD HOLD almost twice the amount of water vapor as air with a **temperature** of 60°F (16°C).

Figure 6-2 Dew point table.

DEW POINT TEMPERATURE °F	WATER VAPOR grams/cubic meters of dry air	TEMPERATURE °F
0	1.31	0
10	2.03	10
20	3.06	20
30	4.53	30
40	6.57	40
50	9.40	50
60	13.33	60
70	18.58	70
80	25.49	80
90	34.49	90
100	46.05	100
110	60.73	110

Imagine that the boxes in Figure 6-3 each represent a cubic meter of air. Each has a temperature of 70°F (21°C) and could hold as much as 18.58 grams of water vapor. In box C, the dew point is also 70°F. So the box contains all the water vapor it possibly can and its *relative humidity* (the actual amount of water vapor divided by the maximum amount of water vapor the air could hold) is 100%. Air in box A has a dew point of 50°F (10°C and so is holding only 9.40 grams of water. Its relative humidity is (9.40/18.58) × 100%, or 51%. Air in box B has a dew point of 60°F (16°C) and contains 13.33 grams of water. Its relative humidity is (13.33/18.58) × 100%, or 72%.

Let's build a simple device for measuring the dew point temperature. Fill a metal bowl or coffee can about one-third full of water at room temperature. To be sure that the water is at the proper temperature, let it stand for about an hour. Then add one ice cube at a time to the container, allowing each cube to completely melt, before adding the next. Gently stir the mixture with an alcohol-in-glass thermometer, occasionally reading the temperature. Look for condensation on the outside of the container. When you see condensation, measure the temperature of the ice-water mixture. This is the dew point temperature! Do not try this if the air temperature is below freezing. Do you know why? Instead, use the ice cube–salt mixture you created in Chapter 5. At what temperature can you get frost to form?

Compare your observation of dew point with that given on your local weather report. Is it the same? Close? Can you compute the dew point temperature if the local weather report gives you only a temperature and a relative humidity? Verify this by using Figure 6.3.

Suppose the reported temperature is 65°F (18°C) and the relative humidity is 75%. What is the dew point? Air at 65°F can hold 15.95 grams of water (exactly midway between the water vapor values at 60°F and 70°F).

Temperature of each box is 70°F

	Amount of water vapor per cubic meter of air	Maximum possible water vapor	Dew point temp.	Relative humidity
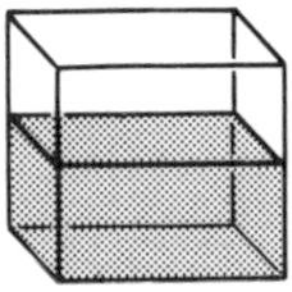 A	9.40 grams	18.58 grams	50 degrees	51%
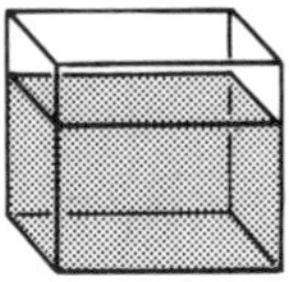 B	13.33 grams	18.58 grams	60 degrees	72%
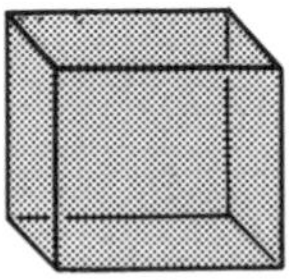 C	18.58 grams	18.58 grams	70 degrees	100%

Figure 6-3. *How relative humidity is computed.*

Since the air is only 75% full of water vapor, multiply the maximum amount of water vapor by the relative humidity percentage to find out the actual water vapor. In this case, 11.96 grams of water vapor are present. Reading along the middle column of the table, this value lies somewhere between 50°F and 60°F. The dew point is actually 56°F.

Provided that you know at least two of the three moisture values—actual water vapor, maximum water vapor possible at a given temperature, and relative humidity percentage—you can compute the third by using this table and some easy mathematics.

Compare temperature, dew point, and relative humidity several times during the day. How do they change? Can you explain why? Relate dew point, temperature, and relative humidity to the presence of clouds, fog, dew, and precipitation. What do you think the relative humidity is inside a cloud? Can it rain when the relative humidity at the ground is not 100%? Can the relative humidity at the ground be 100% when it isn't raining or snowing?

Have a partner hold a cotton ball, and hold another yourself. Assume that each cotton ball represents air at the same temperature. Using a medicine dropper, add one drop of water to one piece of cotton and two drops to the other. Continue to add water in these proportions until one cotton ball starts to "rain." Which one rained first? Why do you think it did?

Cut a sponge into two pieces so that one piece is half the size of the other. The larger sponge represents warmer air, which could hold about twice the amount of water as the smaller sponge. For the example which showed how to compute the relative humidity, the large piece of sponge represents air with a temperature of 70°F; the smaller sponge, a temperature of 50°F. Add several drops of water at a time to each sponge. Which sponge becomes saturated first?

Find three different-size glasses. Arrange these in order of increasing size. Each has a different capacity to hold water, just as air does at different temperatures. Fill the smallest glass with water. Its relative humidity (actual water content divided by maximum amount it can hold) is 100%, similar to what you might find during the early morning. Pour the water into the medium-sized glass. This represents air that has been warmed by the sun. The glass is not full of water, so its relative humidity is below 100%. If there had been dew on the grass, it would have started to evaporate. The largest glass represents air that has been heated considerably by the sun (probably about two o'clock in the afternoon). Pouring the water into this glass results in a relative humidity that is even lower.

Reverse the process, starting with a large glass completely filled with water and pouring all its water into successively smaller glasses. What happens? Hint: this should be done over the kitchen sink.

Clouds: Window to the Sky

CLOUD IDENTIFICATION

Look skyward on a regular basis and try to find lots of different *clouds*. Compare what you see with the descriptions listed below and the photographs and sketches found in Figures 7-1 to 7-7. You may have seen some of these before it rained or snowed; others may have been followed by nice weather. You should now be ready to explore clouds and their environment. All of these clouds occur in the *troposphere*, or the layer of the atmosphere closest to the Earth. The troposphere is typically 30,000 to 70,000 feet (9,000–21,000 m) high.

Clouds

Cirrus. Wispy streamers, waves, or masses of ice crystal clouds at heights of 15,000 feet (4,500 m) or more. Fair-weather clouds unless they thicken into altostratus.

Cirrostratus. A layer of cirrus clouds, usually transparent to sunlight. Fair-weather clouds unless they thicken into altostratus.

Cirrocumulus. Very small cumulus puffs at the cirrus level. These clouds are usually associated with fair weather.

Altostratus. True rain and snow clouds. Bases between 8,000 and 12,000 feet (2,400–3,700 m). Sun may shine dimly through these clouds, or it may be totally hidden.

Altocumulus. Rounded masses of cumulus clouds with bases between 8,000 and 12,000 feet (2400–3700 m). Puffs larger than cirrocumulus. Generally a fair-weather cloud until it occurs with clouds at other levels.

69

Figure 7–1. Cumulus clouds have a "puffy" appearance and are usually associated with fair weather.

Figure 7–2. Altocumulus clouds consist of masses of cumulus clouds.

Figure 7–3. Cirrus clouds often
appear as "streaks."

Figure 7–4. A fog condition created by
stratus clouds touching the ground

Figure 7-5.

Figure 7-6.

Figures 7–5, 7–6, 7–7. Cumulonimbus clouds
cause thunderstorms. This sequence of three
photos shows the formation of a
cumulonimbus cloud. The cloud first
builds vertically, then its top
spreads out across the sky.

Figure 7–7.

Cumulus. Fair-weather clouds that look like cotton puffs and are most often seen during the day. These clouds show rising air currents. Bases are generally 5,000 feet (1,500 m) or lower.

Stratocumulus. These clouds contain more water and have larger puffs than altocumulus, yet generally do not precipitate. Bases around 5,000 feet.

Cumulonimbus. Large, towering cumulus clouds accompanied by thunder, lightning, and rain. Can also bring hail, high winds, and *tornadoes*. Bases between 3,000 and 10,000 feet (900–3,000 m); tops as high as 60,000 feet (18,000 m) or more. Cirrus clouds at the top of the *thunderstorm* can be carried hundreds of miles away from the main thunderstorm cloud. From a distance, the top of a cumulonimbus may look like a blacksmith's anvil.

Stratus. A gray sheet of low clouds within 2,000 feet (600 m) of the ground. Only drizzle or snow grains fall from true stratus clouds. Fog occurs when stratus clouds touch the ground.

Now take an inventory of the sky. Make a list of what you think is there (for example, clouds, airplanes). Ask other family members for their ideas. Categorize your findings.

73

SKY SAFETY

BEFORE beginning any sky activities, realize that sunlight is composed of many different types of energy and radiation. Some of these (like vitamin D) are good for you, and some are bad (*ultraviolet rays* can burn your skin, and the brightness of the sun can hurt your eyes). Even if you have special sunglasses that are supposed to protect your eyes from sunlight, never look directly at the sun. Even at sunrise or sunset, it's only safe to sneak a quick peek.

CLOUD FORMATION

To help you understand how a cloud can be formed, let's make one. Fill a 1- or 2-liter plastic soda bottle about three-fourths full of very warm tap water. Quickly cap the bottle. Gently squeeze and release the bottle. You should see a small cloud appear when you release your pressure; the cloud should disappear when you squeeze again. If the bottle fogs up, just shake it gently. If you can't see the cloud, try shining a flashlight at the upper part of the bottle. Can you explain why the cloud forms and disappears? Clouds are composed of small cloud droplets like these, and may also contain raindrops, snowflakes, ice pellets, and/or hailstones.

The experiment you just performed showed that water vapor can be made to appear as small cloud drops, just by changing the pressure inside the bottle. This is how some clouds form in the atmosphere, too. Because pressure is lower in the upper levels of the atmosphere (there is less weight of air above), rising air can expand, cool, and reach its dew point temperature. But cooling and the presence of water vapor do not necessarily guarantee that a cloud will form. Another ingredient is needed.

Repeat the experiment, with a slight modification. First fill the plastic soda bottle about three-fourths full of very warm tap water. With adult supervision, carefully light a match and blow out the flame. Hold the smoking match near the mouth of the bottle and blow some of the smoke into it. Then drop the match into the bottle and quickly screw on the cap. Again gently squeeze and release the bottle. What do you observe? Is the cloud easier or harder to see? How did the addition of smoke change the cloud formation process?

Try the experiment again, this time with only one-fourth of the bottle filled with water. Did you notice any changes?

Smoke is one of several *condensation nuclei*—particles on which water vapor can condense—which occur in the atmosphere. Dust, volcanic ash, salt spray from the oceans, and even pollutants also serve as condensation nuclei. Watch sunlight shining through a window in your home or watch the sun's rays shining among the trees. What do you observe? At the beach, salt spray can coat your glasses in a few minutes.

The same processes of radiation, conduction, and convection that were involved in energy transfer (Chapter 3) play significant roles in the formation of clouds.

Suppose that air near the ground is cooled to its dew point temperature at night. If conditions are right, you'll not only have dew in the morning but also ground fog. Ground fog is a horizontal or layered (stratus) cloud touching the ground and is usually very shallow (maybe not even as thick as you are tall). With a little heating from the sun, ground fog often evaporates quickly.

Sometimes thick fog may form (Figure 7-4). This often occurs when warm air moves across very cold ground or snow. Fog formed in this way may occur at any time of day and often lasts much longer before it evaporates.

When other layered cloud types such as stratus, altostratus, and cirrostratus form, they usually indicate that a layer of warmer air lies above a layer of colder air.

Whenever warm air lies above cold air, the atmosphere resists up-and-down motions and is called stable. Most cumulus-type clouds occur with convection currents. These rising currents of warmer, less dense air indicate atmospheric instability. As air rises, it expands and cools, eventually reaching its dew point temperature. Since rising air currents often reach their dew point temperature at about the same altitude, cumulus cloud bases are often flat. The tops, which appear to be boiling or bubbling upward, are the rising air currents. If you look carefully, you can often see the cloud tops build upward.

If the upward motion is strong enough, cumulus clouds can grow to great heights, sometimes more than 60,000 feet (18,000 m) above the ground. These clouds, called cumulonimbus, often bring heavy rain, gusty winds, and thunder and lightning. Some cumulonimbus clouds have hail and some even produce tornadoes.

Cumulus clouds usually form during the day. This is because sunlight heats the ground and warms the air from the ground up. The warmer, less dense air near the ground rises. Cumulus clouds tend to disappear by evening as solar energy is lost, the ground starts to cool, and air no longer rises. Study other types of clouds by using the cloud-watching record (Figure 7-8).

To demonstrate convection, make two bubble mixtures, one using very warm water and the other using cold. Go outdoors and blow several bubbles from each mixture. What do you observe? What was the outside air temperature? How did the bubbles behave? Repeat the experiment on a day when the temperature is very different. Was there any change in the way the bubbles floated?

Cumulus clouds can form in other ways. They may develop when air is forced to rise over mountains, and when air near the ground is forced to come together, or converge. The latter happens along weather fronts and

Date Time	Clouds	Direction of Movement*	Other observations: Rain, Snow, descriptions, etc.
sample	Mon. Apr 5 9:30 am	stratus, cirrus altostratus	stratus were still cirrus from west	foggy in low spots; clouds were a dull gray; not very pretty; no rain

*wind direction is estimated by direction FROM which clouds move

Figure 7-8. *Cloud-watching record.*

along sea breeze or lake breeze fronts (where cold air from over the water moves onshore and pushes warmer air away). Do you live near a lake or the ocean? Have you ever visited such places? If so, you may have seen a cumulus cloud line extending along and just inland from the shoreline. You may also have felt the cool winds blowing from the water. Sometimes, especially along the eastern and Gulf coasts of the United States and along the shores of the Great Lakes, you can spend the day at the beach and never get rained on because big thunderstorm clouds stay inland along the sea or lake breeze front.

Although clouds contain billions of water droplets, they don't fall out of the sky. To demonstrate why, run a hair dryer at high speed and aim upward. Place a Ping-

Pong ball within the rising air from the hair dryer. This simulates how cloud droplets and small raindrops stay suspended by updrafts of rising air. Turn the hair dryer to low speed and the ball will fall. If you again run the dryer at high speed, and place a tennis ball in the "updraft," obviously a stronger updraft is needed to keep larger and heavier raindrops suspended. Imagine how strong an updraft is needed to suspend a hailstone the size and weight of a baseball!

CLOUD WATCHING

When cumulus clouds form during the day, you can estimate the height of their bases above the ground (Figure 7-9). Find the dew point temperature (usually given as part of the local weather conditions on The Weather

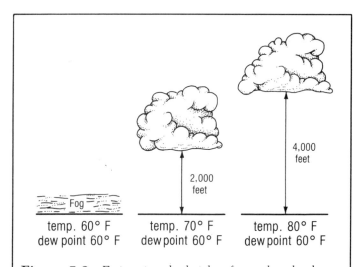

| temp. 60° F | temp. 70° F | temp. 80° F |
| dew point 60° F | dew point 60° F | dew point 60° F |

Figure 7-9. *Estimating the height of cumulus cloud bases using surface temperature and dew point. Notice how cloud bases rise during the day as ground temperatures warm.*

Channel) or measure the dew point using the dew point device that you made in Chapter 6. Subtract the dew point from the current air temperature. For every 1°F, add 200 feet (60 m) to the height of the cloud base. If the difference between temperature and dew point was 18°F (10°C), the cloud base would be about 3,600 feet (1,100 m) above the ground. Check The Weather Channel (if available) for *ceiling* information. The ceiling is the altitude (looking upward from the ground) at which half the sky or more is covered by clouds. When cumulus clouds are present, the ceiling is often the height of the base of these clouds.

Have you ever just lain back on the ground and looked at the shapes, sizes, and movements of clouds (Figure 7-10)? Have you ever seen clouds that looked like dragons? flying elephants? fish? letters of the alphabet? How about other patterns, like lines of clouds or many rows of clouds with clear spaces between them? What about streamers that look like something may be falling from the clouds? Precipitation falling from clouds but not reaching the ground is called *virga*. You can most easily see these when snow showers are in your area or when thunderstorms are nearby. Sometimes you can even see clouds moving from different directions at different altitudes. It is best to watch the clouds move past a stationary object.

Looking for cloud shapes is called nephelococcygia (or "cloud cuckooland"). Cloud patterns tell something about how the clouds were formed.

Drop two small stones into a pond or a puddle. Notice the *wave* patterns that develop. To understand waves, watch the pattern of a jump rope or a Slinky which has been moved up and down at one end. The top of the wave is called its crest or *ridge* and its bottom a valley or a *trough*. You'll hear these words again when television weather reporters talk about the pattern of the jet stream in the atmosphere.

Figure 7–10. *It's a bird; it's a plane; it's a . . . flying elephant??*

Now let's return to our stones in the water. What happens when two wave crests meet? when a crest and a trough meet? The reinforcing and interfering pattern looks very similar to altocumulus clouds. In fact, waves of air moving through the altocumulus layer help to create the patterns we see.

Clouds often transform and actually change from one cloud type to another. The most common transformation occurs when cumulus grows into cumulonimbus. But thunderstorms can rain themselves out, leaving cirrus and altocumulus behind. And sometimes altocumulus clouds, composed of water droplets, transform to snowy streamers that look like cirrus. Have you seen other clouds change their appearance?

Have you ever seen *condensation trails (CON-TRAILS)* left behind by high-altitude aircraft? These are caused when hot, moist exhaust from aircraft engines is quickly chilled. Temperatures are around −30°F (−34°C) at aircraft altitude. Sometimes the CONTRAILS disappear quickly. At other times they grow and spread across the sky. Under which of these conditions do you usually see cirrus clouds? What does this tell you about the amount of moisture in the air at high altitudes?

One way to enjoy the sky is to view it through your own sky or cloud "windows" (Fig. 7-11). Cut out the center of an 8½-by-11-inch (20 by 28 cm) piece of white poster board, leaving a 2- to 3-inch (5–8 cm) rectangular frame. Get paint chips representing different sky or cloud colors (blues, grays, pinks, etc.) from a local paint or hardware store and paste along the frame. You can make a window using poster paint and a wax-paper palette. Place some white paint on the palette. Start with white in the upper left corner of the board. Add a single drop of blue to the white. Mix thoroughly, and paint a 2-inch (5-cm) area to the right of the white on the poster board. Repeat the procedure until the frame of the sky window is completely painted. Allow to dry.

Figure 7–11. You can skywatch by taking
photographs or using "cloud panes."
Make cloud panes out of construction
paper or paint samples (available at
paint stores) and record your observations.

Then repeat on the other side for the grays. Go outside and watch the sky through your personal "cloud and sky window." Match the colors on your window with what you see in the sky.

FORECASTING

Clouds and the sequence of different cloud types that march across the sky often provide important clues about upcoming weather. Explorers and sailors of the past 500 years learned how to read the sky and make fairly accurate weather forecasts. But their forecasting abilities were tempered by two factors. They did not understand the processes which formed clouds, and they did not know how clouds fit together to make weather systems (those lows and fronts that you see on weather maps). Nevertheless, they transferred their observations through the ages by folklore, rhymes, and sayings. Clouds were actually named and classified around 1800 by Luke Howard, an English chemist.

Although there are general forecasting rules based on clouds, these rules can be influenced by local terrain and topography, as well as variations in weather patterns and systems. A few of the more useful rules are described below and are based on cloud sequences often seen with warm and cold fronts. But you should make your own observations and rules for more exact forecasts in your local area. For help, find an "old-timer" who used to spend a lot of time outdoors (for example, a farmer, boater, forester, pilot) and learn about how he or she forecast the weather by watching the sky.

Weather folklore includes rules based on clouds, animal behavior, or legends. Here are a few for you to consider. We've placed a star next to those which have a meteorological basis and are most often true. Can you explain why? Can you add to this list?

- Groundhog sees its shadow, is frightened, and returns to hibernation. Winter will last six more weeks.
- Red sky at night, sailor's delight (good weather is coming tomorrow); red sky in morning, sailor take warning. *
- When clouds appear like rocks and towers, the Earth's refreshed by frequent showers. *
- When the wind is in the east, it is neither good for man nor beast. *
- With dew before midnight, the next day will surely be bright. *
- The more cloud types present, the greater the chance of rain or snow. *
- When high- and/or middle-level clouds move from the south and southwest, precipitation is more likely. *
- Precipitation is more likely to occur when clouds at different levels move from different directions. *
- With mare's tails, tall ships carry low sails.
- A ring around the sun or moon, means rain or snow coming soon (usually). *

Sky photography can be an exciting hobby. Make a sky photography album, being sure to keep a record of when you take pictures and the weather that follows. This is how many meteorologists learned about clouds and the weather they bring. Be especially cautious when taking lightning photographs. It is best to take these from a distance and from a safe place indoors.

You might also try keeping a video cloud album. Place your video camera in a fixed position and use the animate function or alternatively press the run button every 5 seconds to take very short segments of footage. A 20-minute taping translates to about 2 minutes of showing in time-lapse mode. If you can't make your own time-lapse videotape, watch local television weather reports. Some stations have "sky-cams" which show time-lapse cloud motion.

Clouds can modify the daily temperature range. At night, they will often trap heat, making for warmer minimum temperatures. Clouds during the day can often lower the high temperatures. Compare and contrast the daily temperature range and the amount of cloud cover for your area for a week or a month. Tabulate and/or graph your data. What effect do clouds have on the temperatures where you live?

Clouds often restrict our vertical visibility, just as fog restricts our ability to see horizontally. What other things in the atmosphere can limit our horizontal visibility? What was the weather like on days when you could not see very far? When you could see long distances? Why do you think visibility is important? Think about airplane pilots, boaters, and people driving cars and trucks.

Using a detailed highway map centered on your area, locate key landmarks (such as buildings, television towers, mountains) and determine their distance from you. Can you see them? If so, the visibility is at least that distance. When you take a drive with your family, measure visibility. Note where you can first see a significant landmark along the road you are traveling. Use the odometer to measure the distance to that object. That distance is the approximate visibility.

OTHER SKY PHENOMENA

The sky is blue and clouds are usually white, gray, or black. This is all tied to how sunlight interacts with air and water molecules in the sky. Sunlight contains all colors. However, when it strikes air molecules, the blues get scattered the most. That's why our sky looks blue.

When sunlight shines on clouds, some passes through and some is reflected back to space. That's why space shuttle astronauts and weather satellites can see white clouds across the Earth. The more sunlight that is reflected back to space, the darker the bottom of the cloud looks to us. Usually the thicker clouds, and the ones with the most rain or snow, are darker because they block the most sunlight. Thunderstorm clouds, often more than 40,000 feet (12,000 m) tall, are the darkest on the bottom. Watch clouds during the day and on moonlit nights to see these basic cloud colors and how clouds block incoming light. Sometimes sunlight may shine through the thinner edges of a cloud, making the cloud appear to have a "silver lining."

To prove that light contains all colors, you'll need either a plastic bicycle reflector, a prism, or a cut-crystal ball. Hold any of these in sunlight (you may have to turn them somewhat) and you should see the colors of the *spectrum*. If you have a garden hose or a plant mister, spray these outside on a sunny day, with the sun behind you. With about a 40-degree angle between the sun and the water spray and you, you should be able to see a rainbow. Now look for rainbows in the sky. To make the needed angle, the sun must be fairly low in the sky. Rainbows are rare other than near sunrise and sunset, except for places at high latitudes.

You can look for other unusual weather-related optical phenomena. *Sun dogs* are bright colored spots in cirrus clouds at the three and nine o'clock positions relative to the sun. A *halo* is a ring that surrounds the sun or moon. *Crepuscular rays* are the rays of the sun that seem to sneak out from behind clouds.

Stormy
Weather

Stormy weather means different things to different people. While most people have experienced thunderstorms of varying degrees of severity, relatively few have seen a tornado. Almost every winter, strong winds called Chinooks damage houses and cars in parts of Colorado and Wyoming. Along the Gulf and Atlantic coasts, hurricanes are a major danger, but such storms may be infrequent visitors to a particular location. In Arizona, flooding from distant thunderstorms can sometimes strike almost without warning. What are some of the weather hazards that affect your area? How often do they occur? How severe are they? Do they affect small or large areas? Which of these have you experienced? Which have other family members, relatives, or friends experienced?

THUNDERSTORMS

Since *thunderstorms* are the most common weather hazard, we'll begin with them. You are already familiar with thunderstorm clouds. Recall how thunderstorms form. Rapidly rising air allows raindrops to grow by accretion. The updrafts keep the raindrops suspended. Finally the air becomes so filled with large raindrops that the updraft can no longer support them. As they start to fall, downdrafts begin in the thunderstorm. These downdrafts also contain colder air that sinks even faster. What do you think happens when the downdraft reaches the ground?

Take a transparent, plastic sweater or shoe box and fill it two-thirds full of warm tap water. Allow the water to come to rest. Slowly pour a small amount of cold milk into the corner of the box. Look through the side of the box to see what happens. The wedge shape that the milk produces simulates a cold front. In fact, nearly all thunderstorms have such miniature cold fronts. This front separates the colder air underneath the thunderstorm from the warmer air surrounding it (Figure 8-1).

Take advantage of the next time a thunderstorm approaches to verify this. Do you feel the cold outrush of wind as the storm approaches? If you don't experience the wind, you may be on the wrong side of the storm. If you experience very strong winds, you are perhaps being struck by a strong downdraft called a *downburst* or a *microburst* (a small downburst).

Did you see any unusual cloud formations? Did the clouds take on different colors? Did any hail fall? *Hail* forms in thunderstorms when raindrops are caught in a series of updrafts and downdrafts. The hail alternately freezes and melts, while adding to its watery skin. For hail to come from a thunderstorm, updrafts must be very strong.

TORNADOES

Sometimes thunderstorms can produce tornadoes. Have you ever seen a *tornado* from a distance? on television? Has your home ever been struck by one? What does a tornado look like?

Create your own tornado using a clear plastic or glass bottle with a screw-on cap. Fill the bottle three-fourths full of water and cap it. Hold the bottle upside down

Figure 8–1. Cold milk in warm water
simulates a downdraft or microburst
in a thunderstorm. Notice how the colder,
denser fluid sinks to the bottom
and spreads out in a wedge shape.

and create a circular motion with your wrist. What do you notice? Now add less than a drop of any dishwashing detergent to the bottle. Repeat the experiment. What changes? If there are too many bubbles, dilute the solution and try again. For fun, add some Micro-Mini-Machines or other miniature objects that will sink to the bottom of the bottle.

Fill a tall, clear cylindrical container (such as a tennis ball canister) two-thirds full of water. Place a golf ball, Micro-Mini-Machines, or other objects in it. Use a spoon and stir only the upper inch or two of the water in a counterclockwise direction. What happens to the objects at the bottom of the container? This is how tornadoes are able to pick things up.

Imagine a tornado spinning across the ground with wind speeds between 75 and 300 mph (120–480 kph). As the tornado moves (sometimes with a forward speed as fast as 60 mph, or 95 kph), strong winds blow against houses, trees, and other objects with great force. Suddenly the wind comes from a different direction, applying new forces. What do you think happens when such changeable forces act on an object? It is these forces and the flying debris that cause damage to buildings. Pressure differences between the tornado and the surrounding air do not cause buildings to explode!

While all buildings are at risk from tornado and downburst winds, mobile homes are especially vulnerable. Lay an empty cereal box on the edge marked "ingredients" on your kitchen table. Place the box so that its bottom is facing toward you. Blow hard. Were you able to blow the box over? Now move so that you are facing the front of the box; in the atmosphere this would be a wind blowing from a different direction. Again, blow hard. What was different? Can you explain why mobile homes are so easily damaged by high winds? What are some things you could do to be safe from tornadoes?

LIGHTNING

Do all thunderstorms have *lightning?* Do you hear *thunder* every time you see lightning? What does lightning look like? Is it always bright, or is it sometimes hidden by the clouds? Some lightning travels between clouds; other lightning moves between the clouds and the ground.

Lightning occurs when positive and negative charges in raindrops, hailstones, and snowflakes become separated. These charges group themselves within the cumulonimbus cloud and on the ground near it. When too much charge accumulates in different places, the charges try to balance themselves. For this to happen, electricity must flow from one charge group to another. What results is a giant spark called lightning. You can hear the effects of lightning by listening for crackling or static on an AM radio station.

You may have seen "lightning" on a smaller scale (static electricity) in your home, especially on days when the dew point was low. Clothes sometimes stick together in the clothes dryer or when you wear them. And if you shuffle your stockinged feet across a carpet and then touch a metal doorknob, you may get zapped.

One way to see how positive and negative charges can be separated is to use black pepper and a charged balloon. Sprinkle some pepper on a plate. Blow up a balloon and charge it by rubbing it over your hair. Look in a mirror to see what happens when you hold the balloon near your hair. Next, hold the balloon directly over the plate and slowly move it toward the pepper. What happens?

Add some water to the plate and float some pepper on it. Wipe the pepper off the balloon. Recharge the balloon by rubbing it in your hair. Bring the balloon toward the pepper. What moved? Can you explain why?

Turn on the cold water faucet at your kitchen sink and get a small, steady stream of water. Again recharge the balloon. Bring the balloon toward the water. What occurred? What did you think would happen? Make the water stream bigger and repeat the experiment.

Although raindrops can grow by accretion, electric charge differences in a thunderstorm allow the raindrops to grow even bigger.

Use a pin and pop your balloon. You've just made thunder. Can you explain how? Think about how thunder is made in the atmosphere. Lightning is very hot, sometimes even hotter than the sun. The lightning rapidly heats the air it passes through, causing the air to expand. Cooling follows quickly and the air contracts. What does this do to the air next to the lightning?

Compare the different types of lightning and the shapes of the flashes with the sound of thunder that follows. Which type of lightning makes low rumbles? Which type of lightning creates loud cracks? Is there lightning that doesn't make thunder? Some people think there is and call it "heat lightning," but what they don't realize is that the lightning is too far away for them to hear the thunder.

Lightning travels faster than sound (186,000 miles, or 299,000 km, per second for light compared to slightly more than 1,000 feet, or 300 m, per second for sound), so you see lightning before you hear thunder. How could you use this difference to estimate how far away the lightning was? Remember that you see the lightning almost instantaneously and that the distance you estimate can be anywhere on a sphere that encircles you. It does not have to be measured horizontally from where you are.

Why do you think lightning is dangerous? Can you develop a list of things that you and your family can do to be safe from lightning?

FLOODING

Flooding is an extreme case of the accumulation phase of the water cycle. It happens when (1) too much rain falls too quickly on an area and/or (2) the rain cannot be absorbed or run off fast enough. Take any container and fill it up with water from your kitchen tap, timing the fill-up. The first time, fill the container slowly. Then fill it quickly. What do you notice?

Next fill each of three 6-ounce paper cups half full of sand, soil, and clay, respectively. Pack the contents of each firmly. Measure out three 1-ounce (28-g) water samples and pour one of these into each cup at about the same time. Which one enters the ground most quickly? Add a second 1-ounce cup of water to each. What would happen if a heavy thunderstorm passed over an area with a lot of concrete and asphalt? What if several storms passed over the same area in a short period of time?

Remove any excess water from the cups and invert them on a cookie sheet or large pan. Remove the cups, but leave your "mountains." Measure out three 1-ounce cups of water, one for each mountain. Make it rain on each mountain using a medicine dropper. What do you observe? What could be done to lessen the amount of runoff and *erosion?* Look around your home and neighborhood for evidence of erosion. After a rain, watch how water moves down a street into storm drains and drainage ditches.

Sometimes flooding occurs at great distances from where the rain that caused it actually fell. In the western United States, especially in Arizona and New Mexico, rain falling from thunderstorms over mountains can race down dry washes, gullies, and arroyos, creating flooding even where skies are clear. In flat areas, anywhere in the world, rivers can merge as they flow downstream and create widespread flooding, days and even weeks after rain falls. Such flooding may take several days to subside.

While thunderstorms create a lot of flooding, there are other causes. These include winter rains falling on frozen ground or melting snow, ice blocks that dam a river, dam failures, and heavy rains from hurricanes and other ocean storms.

Watch television news and weather reports and read newspapers to learn about flooding which occurs around the world. What are the impacts and dangers to people, animals, and property from flooding? What can be done to lessen these?

Compare the force of moving water with that of wind. Do you understand why you should be careful not to get caught in moving water? Think about what could happen if a car were caught in it. What would happen if moving water, (in the form of waves), were to crash ashore during a period of high winds?

HURRICANES

Television weather reports during the summer and fall often contain information about *tropical cyclones* (the name given to all hurricanes and tropical storms). Although attention is usually focused on cyclones in the Atlantic Ocean, Gulf of Mexico, and Caribbean Sea (these storms most often strike the United States), you'll also hear about *hurricanes* in the eastern Pacific Ocean, *typhoons* in the western Pacific, and *cyclones* near Australia and in the Indian Ocean (Figure 8-2).

Tropical cyclones are classified according to wind speed as shown in the Saffir-Simpson hurricane scale (Figure 8-3). These winds are related to the central pressure of the storm, the height of wind-driven waves, *storm surge,* and the potential for damage in coastal areas.

To simulate a hurricane's circulation, fill a large bowl

Figure 8–2. Weather satellite photo of Hurricane Hugo approaching the South Carolina coast. The 1989 hurricane devastated large areas of the southeastern states.

about two-thirds full of water. Stir the water in a counterclockwise direction and then remove the stirrer. Place a small amount of cooking oil on top of the spinning water. What do you see? This shape is similar to the symbol used by meteorologists worldwide to represent hurricanes on weather maps. It's also similar to what a hurricane looks like on a weather satellite picture.

If you can, visit a beach and study sand dunes. How

HURRICANE CLASSIFICATION
Scale used by the National Weather Service

Saffir–Simpson hurricane intensity scale

Category	Pressure	Winds	Surge	Damage
1	28.94″ or more	74–95 mph	4–5 feet	Minimal
2	28.50–28.91″	96–110 mph	6–8 feet	Moderate
3	27.91–28.47″	111–130 mph	9–12 feet	Extensive
4	27.17–27.88″	131–155 mph	13–18 feet	Extreme
5	27.17″ or less	Over 155 mph	Over 18 feet	Catastrophic

Figure 8-3. *Tropical cyclones are classified according to the Saffir-Simpson scale.*

do you think they were formed? The dunes help protect inland areas from the forces of the ocean. Are the dunes protected from people? What, if anything, is growing on the dunes?

How can the dunes be destroyed? Watch the white caps on the water. At what wind speed do white caps usually first appear? To see the impact of waves on the beach, build a small sand castle near the water. How could you protect your castle from the waves? Compare the kinds of barriers you would provide for a sand castle to beach barriers which occur naturally and to concepts used by humans to protect or reclaim beach areas.

Rising water, along with wind-driven waves, can be devastating along a coastal area. But how does the ocean water rise to create the deadly storm surge?

First, fill a cookie sheet half full with water. In one corner, place several drops of blue food coloring. Put yellow, red and green colors in each of the other corners. Hold a hair dryer about 2 feet (0.6 m) from the cookie sheet. At low speed, blow air from one corner of the sheet toward an adjacent corner. What happens?

Invert a glass in a bowl of water. Hold your finger over one end of a length of plastic tubing. Run the tubing from outside the bowl into the water and into the inverted glass so that it extends above the water level. Remove your finger. Slowly suck air out from the glass to represent the lower pressure in a hurricane. What happens to the water level?

Look at a map showing coastal bays (for example, Narragansett Bay, Rhode Island; Mobile Bay, Alabama; and Tampa Bay, Florida). Compare the shape of these bays to the corners of a cookie sheet. Place 2 ounces (57 g) of water on the cookie sheet. Over a sink, gently tilt the sheet so the water runs toward a corner. What happens to the depth of the water?

You've now seen the ways that wind, pressure, and coastal geography can act to increase the height of water in a hurricane (or in other strong ocean storms).

Although geographic positions of tropical cyclones are reported as a point, it is important to realize that these storms can be hundreds of miles across. Keep in mind that strong winds, heavy rains, and flooding of evacuation routes can occur well before the center of the hurricane reaches the coast. Local officials will often try to evacuate people in low-lying coastal areas as much as a day before the hurricane is expected to strike.

On a hurricane tracking chart (see sample, Figure 8-4), keep track of tropical cyclones in the news. Plot positions given in television news and weather reports every twenty-four hours. Use extrapolation to predict where you think the storm will be the next day. Compare your forecast with that of the National Hurricane Center. Notice when watches, warnings, and evacuation information is given.

It's rare for tropical cyclones to strike California,

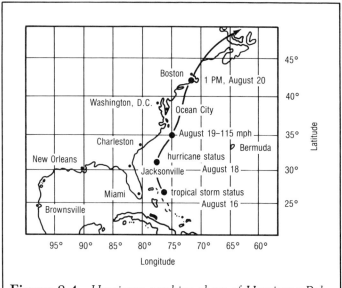

Figure 8-4. *Hurricane tracking chart of Hurricane Bob (1991).*

England, and Chile. Yet, places like Bangladesh, Mexico, the United States Gulf Coast, and Japan have frequent encounters. Think about where and when tropical cyclones develop. What ingredients are needed for them to form? What causes tropical cyclones to weaken and die? Sometimes tropical cyclones, or the low-pressure system that remains after they weaken, affect parts of the central United States, Arizona, and the Appalachian Mountains. What types of weather would these systems bring as they move toward inland areas? If your library has a newspaper microfilm archive, study storms like Camille (August 14–22, 1969), Gilbert (September 8–19, 1988), and Hurricane Hugo (September 16–24, 1989).

WINTER STORMS

Winter storms come in all shapes and sizes. Some bring very cold rain, even to places like Arizona or north Florida. Some bring freezing rain that coats trees, cars, and roads with an icy glaze. Others bring heavy snow. All can bring strong winds and varying combinations of winter weather conditions. It's this variability, which often occurs over small distances, that makes forecasting these storms so difficult (Figure 8-5).

Trace weather map features (highs, lows, fronts, clouds, and precipitation) from your local newspaper weather map onto a piece of clear acetate. Add expected wind direction at several places. Overlay this weather map onto a map of your state, centering a low-pressure system over your city. What is the weather like 20 miles (32 km) to your north? 20 miles to the south? Move the low-pressure center to your north; to your south. What happens to your weather? Now overlay the weather map on a U.S. map, again centered on your area. Compare weather conditions across a larger geographical region.

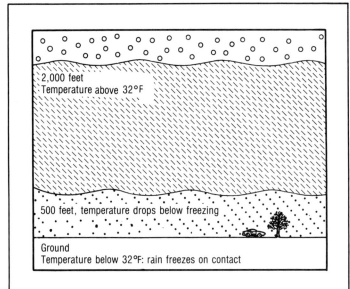

2,000 feet
Temperature above 32°F

500 feet, temperature drops below freezing

Ground
Temperature below 32°F: rain freezes on contact

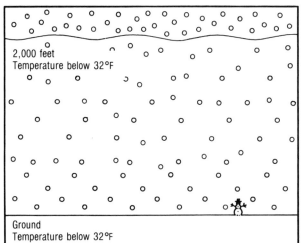

2,000 feet
Temperature below 32°F

Ground
Temperature below 32°F

Figure 8-5. *The presence of a layer of warm air several hundred feet above the ground can turn snow to rain. The rain will freeze on contact with surfaces colder than 32°F.*

Move the weather system map across the United States from southwest to northeast, just as a jet stream might move it. Start over the Texas panhandle, near Amarillo, and move the system toward Chicago, Illinois. What would the weather sequence be at places like Omaha, Nebraska, and St. Louis, Missouri? Notice how long it rains or snows in Omaha.

Move the low-pressure system on different tracks and see what the weather would be at different places. Where should the low-pressure system pass by to give a place the best chance of a major snowstorm? thunderstorms and possibly tornadoes? Modify the precipitation types based on temperatures and season.

Freezing rain occurs when warm raindrops fall through a very shallow layer of cold air. They don't freeze until they strike something near the ground (for example, trees, cars, grass) that is cold, glazing objects like a coating of icing on a cake. *Sleet* forms when warm rain falls through a thicker layer of cold air and becomes small ice pellets before it reaches the ground (Figure 8-6).

Lake effect snows occur around the Great Lakes, the Great Salt Lake in Utah, and other larger, nonfrozen lakes. These are very localized areas of heavy snowfall, with nearby areas receiving little or none. Three factors contribute to their occurrence. Cold, dry air passes over these lakes in fall and early winter and picks up heat and moisture. This makes the air unstable and allows cumulus-type clouds to form. As the clouds move onto the shore at the opposite side of the lake, they are forced to rise by two factors. One involves air being forced up nearby hills and mountains. The other occurs because winds over land are weaker than those over water. Friction slows down wind more over land than water. Air converges at low levels near the shore. If the wind blows the cumulus clouds along the length of the lake for a long period of time, localized snows can be measured in feet (Figure 8-7)!

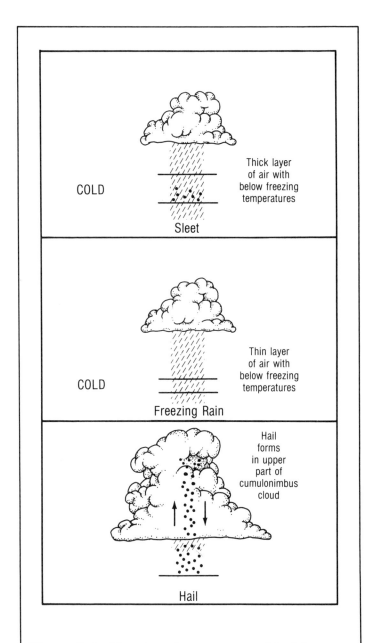

COLD

Thick layer
of air with
below freezing
temperatures

Sleet

COLD

Thin layer
of air with
below freezing
temperatures

Freezing Rain

Hail
forms
in upper
part of
cumulonimbus
cloud

Hail

Figure 8-6. *How sleet, freezing rain, and hail form.*

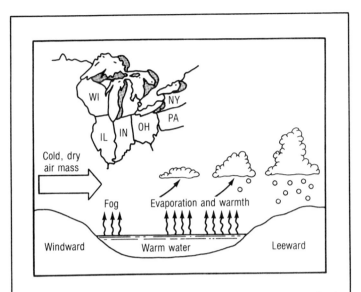

Figure 8-7. *The formation of "lake-effect" snows. Such snows are most likely to occur in shaded locations.*

Winter weather dangers are many. Ice and snow are slippery, making it difficult to drive cars or walk safely. Deep snow or a blinding snowstorm can maroon cars and people. If you were trapped in a car in such a snowstorm, what would you do to protect yourself? What would you include in a car's winter-weather safety kit for such circumstances?

WATCHES, WARNINGS, AND ADVISORIES

To help you prepare for the weather hazards described in this chapter, you should be familiar with the terminology of watches, warnings, and *advisories* issued by the National Weather Service (NWS). However, NWS forecasters and their arsenal of observing equipment are not infallible; sometimes storms can strike with little or no warning. Being a keen observer can often help you recognize these weather events on your own.

When there is a possibility that a dangerous storm could occur, the NWS will issue a *watch*. This means "watch out," listen to radio and television for additional information, and think about what you would do if a warning follows. A watch for a hurricane may be issued more than a day ahead of when the storm is expected; for tornadoes, you may receive a watch only a few hours ahead.

A *warning* means that the storm is either happening nearby or that it is almost certain to occur in your area in a short while. For hurricanes, a twelve- to twenty-four-hour advance warning may be given; for tornadoes, it may be only minutes.

If there are hazardous travel conditions such as icy roads, snow, fog, or blowing dust, local information may be given to radio and television stations. Special forecasts and advisories are also provided for boaters, pilots, forest-fire fighters, and people concerned with avalanches.

Although winter weather can be dangerous, it can also be fun. Think about what winter would be like if you couldn't ski, ice-skate, build snow forts, or have snowball fights.

Weather
in Your
Life

NEW ENGLAND SNOWSTORM SHUTS
DOWN SCHOOLS

WATER RATIONING SLATED FOR SOUTHERN CALIFORNIA
AS DROUGHT ENTERS SIXTH YEAR

HURRICANE SLAMS INTO GULF COAST

ENERGY PRICES SOAR DURING RECORD
COLD SPELL

Newspaper headlines like these show some of the ways that weather affects us. Can you find other headlines to add to these? Scenes in movies and books are often set by weather. The clothing we wear, the foods we eat, the recreational activities we do, and the moods we experience are all tied to the weather. Take a minute or two and make a list of all the equipment and accessories in your family car that are weather related. Can you think of other ways that weather affects us? Talk about the influence of weather with other family members.

Weather not only affects us, it affects our environment. Certain weather patterns can cause pollutants to collect in the lower levels of the atmosphere. Wind can blow smoke, dust, and volcanic ash far away from their source region. Weather patterns can even affect how rocks weather and soil erodes and how your trash can *decompose*.

WEATHERING

How much garbage and trash do you create each week? Weigh yourself. Then weigh yourself holding your garbage bag at the end of a week. Most garbage is collected every day or couple of days. How much garbage is accumulated in your neighborhood, city, county, and state each week? Think about the impact of this on landfills and garbage processing plants.

Contact the company that collects your garbage. Find out how much they collect in a day. Have they ever analyzed the percentage of the garbage that decomposes (that is, is *biodegradable*)? Using gloves, carefully separate your garbage and trash into several categories, including metals, glass, plastics, papers, and biodegradables. If your area has a recycling program, contact them for information, too.

To demonstrate the effect of *weathering* on a landfill, take three each of the following: rubber bands, pieces of a plastic grocery bag, pieces of a paper grocery bag, parts of a cardboard egg carton or cereal box, pieces of aluminum foil, and parts of a Styrofoam cup. Place one of the rubber bands in an empty container, another in a container with soil, and the third in a container with water. Do the same with each trio of other objects. Make sure that all the objects placed in the soil container are buried in the soil. Place all containers in a sunny place and leave them there for a month. When you return, examine all of the material in each container. What broke apart or became weathered? What didn't? How long do you think it would take for some of the objects to decompose?

Repeat the experiment trying different ways to speed up decomposition. Try alternately freezing and thawing the containers, adding heat to the containers, and grinding or tearing up the materials before adding them to the containers. Compare this process to what happens to rocks, sidewalks, and highways.

AIR POLLUTION

What is *air pollution*? If it is measured in your area, find out how and what the *air quality* readings mean. Keep track of air quality readings for a month. Graph your data. Is there a relationship between air quality and day of the week (in other words, number of cars on the road)? Air quality and weather (windy versus calm)? Why do you think air pollution is so bad in places like Los Angeles, California, Denver, Colorado, and Washington, D.C.? What weather conditions would make air quality better? What can businesses do to reduce air pollution? What can you and your family do? How do plants and trees help to reduce air pollution?

Observe smokestacks, if there are any in your neighborhood. What comes out of them? Do you think it is hot or cold? Why does the smoke sometimes rise vertically and sometimes spread out horizontally? Think about stability of the atmosphere. Why do you think smoke stacks are built so high?

What if there were a chemical or nuclear accident near your town? How would weather affect the movement and concentration of gases inside the toxic pollution cloud? Read about the Chernobyl nuclear power plant accident in Russia in 1986. How far away from the plant was the environment affected? How do you think forest fires, volcanoes, and sewage treatment plants affect the atmosphere?

We know that outside air is often "polluted." What types of pollutants may be present in the air inside your home? your school? where your parents work?

To supply our homes, factories, schools, and businesses with electricity, power companies have to generate it. These power plants can convert coal, oil, wind, and water power—and even nuclear energy—into electricity. Learn about these conversion processes and determine some of the benefits and risks of each type. Each process creates heat. What do the power companies do to get rid of this heat?

ACID RAIN

News reports often talk about *acid rain*. What does "acid rain" mean? How acid is the rain where you live? And does it vary from one rain day to another? from one season to another?

The pH scale, developed by a Danish biochemist, is used to classify the acidity of solutions. Distilled water has a pH of about 7.0; unpolluted rainwater has a pH around 5.6; lemon juice has a pH of about 2.0.

You can measure the acidity of rainwater by using special test kits or by making your own indicator juice. Carefully cut up a head of red cabbage and drop it into boiling water. Once it has cooked, carefully remove the cabbage leaves and let the red cabbage juice cool. Place the juice in a sealed container in your refrigerator until the next rainy day.

After you collect rainwater, line up six small glasses. Put 5 tablespoons of red cabbage juice into each. Add rainwater to one glass. Then add equal amounts of milk of magnesia (pH between 10 and 11), milk (pH approximately 6.6), apple juice (pH around 3.0), and lemon juice (pH around 2.0) to four of the other glasses. In the last glass, add an equal amount of distilled water (pH of 7.0). You don't have to buy it, just boil some water and allow it to cool before placing it in the glass. Compare the color of the glass with the rainwater to the colors of the other glasses. The closest match provides a relative measure of the acidity of the rain.

Then measure the pH of household liquids and powders (such as soda, vinegar, shampoo, laundry detergent, tap water).

In small containers, plant fast-growing seeds (radish or bean, for example). Initially treat these as you would any plant, watering sparingly and placing in a warm, sunny location. Once the plants have sprouted, begin watering selected plants with the different liquids and powders you tested above. What effect do these have on the plants? What effect do you think acid rain might have on trees? On acid-loving plants such as azaleas and rhododendrons?

ENERGY

Conduct an energy survey in your home. Where is heat lost in winter? Gained in summer? Check around windows, doors, walls, and ceilings. Measure the insulation in your attic, if you have one. After a snowstorm, watch how snow melts off your roof and those of your neighbors. What might account for the differences you see? Check with your local energy company and ask for information about saving energy in your home.

Degree-days are a measure of energy use. To determine the number of degree-days, use the worksheet in Figure 9-1 to compute the average temperature each day. Compare this value to 65°F. The difference between the two values is the number of degree-days. For example, if the high temperature was 58°F and the low temperature was 42°F, the average temperature for the day would be 50°F. Subtracted from 65°F, this yields 15 heating degree-days. This means that a certain amount of energy would be required to heat your home to bring it to a comfortable 65°F temperature. Similarly, average temperatures above 65°F result in a need for cooling; hence we use the term "cooling degree-days."

Date	Meter Reading	24-Hour Energy Use	Temperatures*			Degree Days**	Remarks
			High	Low	Avg.		
Mon 10/25 8:00 A.M.	54665	-----	-----	-----	-----	-----	-----
Tue 10/26 8:20 A.M.	54734	69	62	46	54	heating 11	A.M. sun P.M. clouds
degree-day formulas		heating degree day = 65 − $\dfrac{(\text{high} + \text{low temperature})}{2}$					
Thu 7/14 6:25 A.M.	01090	cooling degree day = $\dfrac{(\text{high} + \text{low temperature})}{2}$ − 65					
Fri 7/15 6:25 A.M.	01175	85	97	79	88	23	humid few clouds
Sat 7/16 7:25 A.M.	01277	102	100	77	88.5	23.5	record heat 4 washes
Sun 7/17 6:25 A.M.	01381	104	104	81	92.5	27.5	whew! more record heat
Mon 7/18 6:25 A.M.	01479	98	100	78	89	24	late afternoon t-storm
Tue 7/19 6:25 A.M.	01576	97	94	75	84.5	19.5	humid late PM t-storm
Wed 7/20 6:25 A.M.	01655	79	95	74	84.5	19.5	air cond set to lower temp; aftn ⚡
Thu 7/21 6:25 A.M.	01732	77	92	76	84	19	lots of A.M. clouds 5 P.M. heavy ⚡
Fri 7/22 6:25 A.M.	01807	75	90	72	81	16	lots of clouds; windy eve ☔/⚡
Sat 7/23 6:40 A.M.	01891	84	Fri. 85	Sat. 73	79	14	cloudy-no rain laundry, shower & dishwasher day
Sun 7/24 6:25 A.M.	01949	58	85	69	77	12	cloudy all day noon high temp very heavy ⚡ in P.M.

*For energy meter readings in the evening, use current day's low and high temperatures. For energy meter readings in the morning, use yesterday's high and current day's low temperatures.

**use colors or other code to separate heating from cooling degree days.

Figure 9-1. *Sample degree-day worksheet.*

Determine which energy source is being used to heat or cool your home. Then read that meter at the same time each day to determine daily energy use. Compare daily energy use and degree-days.

You can also compare energy use for a month with the total number of daily degree-days for the same period. Check your gas or electric bills to see if your power company gives you degree-day information.

Place your thermometer inside the family car, but not in direct sunlight. Be sure the car is in a sunny location. Roll up all the windows and leave your thermometer there for about an hour. Predict what you think the thermometer reading will be when you return. How high was the temperature inside the car? You have just simulated the *greenhouse effect* using car windows, which trap heat much as do windows in a greenhouse. This same greenhouse effect operates when sunlight enters the Earth's atmosphere and is trapped by carbon dioxide, other gases, and clouds. Compare temperatures on cloudy and clear mornings. When is it warmer? Without the greenhouse effect, life on Earth would be impossible. Think about how you can use the greenhouse effect to warm and cool your home and yourself.

RELATIVE HUMIDITY

Relative humidity (see Chapter 6) can make us feel warmer or colder than we would normally feel because of the actual air temperature. If the air is very dry, rapid evaporation from our skin chills us. If it is very humid, we perspire, but the water stays on our skin, unable to cool us by evaporating. How do you feel when it is very humid or very dry outside?

In the winter, our homes are normally extremely dry. Sometimes the relative humidity drops to below 10%, even drier than it is in some deserts. Any moisture on our skin will quickly evaporate, causing us to feel even colder. The normal response to this is to turn up the heat. But that only lowers the relative humidity, adding to the evaporation process. What could you do to raise the relative humidity value inside your home and make you feel warmer?

Using the dew point table from Chapter 6, let's compute what the relative humidity might be inside your home on several winter days (Figure 9-2).

In the summer, it's the heat and humidity (also referred to as *humiture*), that makes many people feel uncomfortable (Figure 9-3). Some places in the western United States don't have to worry much about humiture. But people east of the Rocky Mountains can experience high humiture values for most of the summer and parts of spring and fall. Arizona has a short period in the summer when it faces high humiture conditions. The humiture table will help you understand how heat and humidity combine to make you feel uncomfortable. Air-conditioning systems not only cool the air; they remove water, thus allowing your body to cool more easily by evaporation.

Our bodies lose heat by conduction, convection, and radiation, as well as evaporation. By wearing multiple layers of lightweight clothing, you'll actually be warmer than by wearing one heavy piece of clothing. Check out skiing, camping, and other outdoor recreational stores for ideas about cold-weather clothing.

But when the wind blows, heat loss from exposed skin can be very rapid. The windchill table (Figure 9-4) shows how cold your exposed skin would feel under different wind and temperature conditions. To determine *windchill temperature*, consult Figure 9-4. A quick way to determine the approximate windchill temperature is to use the following formula:

Windchill temperature = Air temperature − 1.5 × wind speed

• The outside air temperature is 30°F and the relative humidity is 100%. This outside air is brought inside and heated to a warm and toasty 70°F.

What is the relative humidity inside your home?

Actual water vapor content of outside air with a dew point of 30°F is 4.53 gm/m^3.

Maximum water vapor content of inside air at 70°F is 18.58 gm/m^3.

If the outside air is brought inside and heated to 70°F, its relative humidity would be (4.53/18.58) × 100% = 24%.

• Suppose you only heated the outside air to 65°F, instead of 70°F. What is the relative humidity inside your home?

Actual water vapor content of outside air with a dew point of 30°F is 4.53 gm/m^3.

Maximum water vapor content of the inside air at 65°F is only 15.95 gm/m^3.

The indoor relative humidity would be (4.53/15.95) × 100% = 28%

• Suppose the outside air temperature is 30°F and the relative humidity is 29%. This means that the dew point of the outside air is 0°F.

Bring this outside air inside and heat it to a warm and toasty 70°F.

Actual water vapor content of outside air with a dew point of 0°F is 1.31 gm/m^3.

The maximum water vapor content of inside air at 70°F is 18.58 gm/m^3.

If this outside air is brought inside and heated to 70°F, its relative humidity would be (1.31/18.58) × 100% = 7%.

Figure 9-2. *How to calculate indoor relative humidity.*

HUMITURE CHART

Temperature + Humidity = Humiture
(How hot it feels)

Relative Humidity %

Temperature—Fahrenheit	10	20	30	40	50	60	70	80	90
104	98	104	110	120	132				
102	97	101	108	117	125				
100	95	99	105	110	120	132			
98	93	97	101	106	110	125			
96	91	95	98	104	108	120	128		
94	89	93	95	100	105	111	122		
92	87	90	92	96	100	106	115	122	
90	85	88	90	92	96	100	106	114	122
88	82	86	87	89	93	95	100	106	115
86	80	84	85	87	90	92	96	100	109
84	78	81	83	85	86	89	91	95	99
82	77	79	80	81	84	86	89	91	95
80	75	77	78	79	81	83	85	86	89
78	72	75	77	78	79	80	81	83	85
76	70	72	75	76	77	77	77	78	79
74	68	70	73	74	75	75	75	76	77

Figure 9-3. *"Humiture"* = *temperature + humidity. It is a measure of how hot it feels outdoors.*

Windchill Chart

The windchill index, the cooling power of the wind, is only an approximation because how you actually feel will also depend on other variables such as the type of clothing worn, the amount of exposed flesh, and your physical condition at the time.

Temperatures °F

Calm	35	30	25	20	15	10	5	0	−5	−10	−15	−20	−25
5	33	27	21	16	12	7	1	−6	−11	−15	−20	−26	−31
10	21	16	9	2	−2	−9	−15	−22	−27	−31	−38	−45	−52
15	16	11	1	−6	−11	−18	−25	−33	−40	−45	−51	−60	−65
20	12	3	−4	−9	−17	−24	−32	−40	−46	−52	−60	−68	−76
25	7	0	−7	−15	−22	−29	−37	−45	−52	−58	−67	−75	−83
30	5	−2	−11	−18	−26	−33	−41	−49	−56	−63	−70	−78	−87
35	3	−4	−13	−20	−27	−35	−43	−52	−60	−67	−72	−83	−90
40	1	−4	−15	−22	−29	−36	−45	−54	−62	−69	−76	−87	−94
45	1	−6	−17	−24	−31	−38	−46	−54	−63	−70	−78	−87	−94
50	0	−7	−17	−24	−31	−38	−47	−56	−63	−70	−79	−88	−96

Wind speed (miles per hour)

Figure 9-4. *How to find the windchill temperature.*

AGRICULTURE

Temperature, wind, rain (or the lack of it), and amount of sunlight all affect how plants grow. If the weather cooperates, look for "bumper crops." If the weather is bad, crops fail. Check prices of fruits and vegetables in your newspaper's grocery advertisements and at the grocery store. Chart the price of several fruits and vegetables over a period of several months. Choose agricultural products which have widely varying prices due to seasonal factors or lack of availability. Grapes, peppers, asparagus, and lettuce are among the crops with the greatest price fluctuations. Are these foods available throughout the year or only in certain seasons?

In the business pages of your newspaper look for the "futures" prices of oranges, corn, and soybeans. Futures

115

are an indication of what prices may be for certain foods in the near future. Look for news articles that describe why futures prices change.

Trees are also a form of agriculture. How does weather affect trees grown for lumber and for fruit? Will fruit trees flower if it is too warm during the winter?

Lack of rain is a major factor in causing forests and grasslands to dry out. Human carelessness and lightning can ignite these areas, creating serious forest and grass fires. Examine two leaves from a tree or plant, one that's alive and one that has dried out. Wrinkle the leaves in your hand. What do you observe? Compare branches that are dead and dried with those that are still alive.

Are there certain areas of the United States that are more prone to forest and grass fires? Are such fires more common at certain times of the year? Use your answers to help determine other weather factors that can contribute to the drying-out process.

Examine any indoor plants you may have. What causes them to dry out? If you or your neighbors have a Christmas tree, recognize that the tree can dry out in the very dry environment of your home. What can you do to slow the drying-out of Christmas trees?

TECHNOLOGY

Following World War II, weather radar became an important weather tool. *Radar* (short for *radio detection and ranging*) involves the transmission of a radio beam through the atmosphere. During its flight, the beam strikes various objects (trees, mountains, buildings, and precipitation). The energy of the radar beam is absorbed and/or scattered. Some of the energy bounces back to the radar site. There it is processed and displayed on screens, showing where the reflection occurred. The process is much like what happens when you hear an echo. In fact, what the radar "sees" are called "echoes."

Larger raindrops and hailstones reflect the most energy and normally appear as reds and yellows on local television weather displays. Drizzle and snow reflect the least energy. Sometimes unusual temperature patterns in the atmosphere trap the radar beam near the ground. The beam is forced to strike many ground-based objects, producing an entire radar screen filled with "echoes" that don't exist. Your local television meteorologist may refer to this as "ground clutter."

A new radar system, called *Doppler radar*, is now being used by the National Weather Service. Many local television stations also have this radar system. Doppler radar not only detects rain or snowfall, but it also measures the wind toward or away from the radar. This is the same principle that lets you distinguish between sirens that are approaching you from those that are moving away. It's also what the police use to measure the speed of moving cars. Doppler radar systems work even when rain or snow isn't present. They can provide information about severe storms even before they occur and enable meteorologists to provide the public with more accurate warnings.

Weather *satellites* first viewed the Earth's cloud patterns in 1960. Now, they are a key part of weather analysis on a global scale. Polar orbiting satellites travel around the world about once every ninety minutes, scanning high and low latitudes alike. A *geostationary* satellite (called GOES) is fixed above a point on the equator, at an altitude of about 22,000 miles (35,000 km). As the Earth spins on its axis, the satellite remains "locked" over that point. Hence GOES sees the same area all the time. It takes several geostationary satellites to provide a complete view of the Earth's weather. GOES satellites view best within 60 degrees of the equator.

Weather satellites not only show cloud patterns but can be used to locate weather fronts, developing storms, hurricanes, thunderstorms, and fog. In addition to taking visible photographs (of what you would see if you were in the satellite), weather satellites can "see" even at night by taking *infrared* pictures (which show temperatures of clouds and the ground). Techniques have also been developed which allow forecasters to estimate rainfall and snowfall from satellite pictures. New weather satellite instruments help measure high-altitude ozone, volcanic eruptions, and ocean currents. You have probably seen weather satellite picture sequences on TV weather reports. Usually, infrared pictures are shown.

In this chapter, you have seen some of the ways that weather affects us. Sometimes it inconveniences us; at other times it affects us economically. But weather is always a factor to be dealt with.

We can't control weather—at least not yet. But we can all adapt our environment and ourselves to compensate for the weather. What does this mean as far as you, the reader, are concerned? You can dress appropriately, use energy resources more efficiently, be more aware of weather's affect on the environment, and take proper safety measures when severe weather threatens. You can also make an impact at home by showing other family members how they can use weather knowledge in their day-to-day activities.

Glossary

accretion: the growth of a precipitation particle by the collision of an ice crystal or snowflake with a supercooled water droplet that freezes upon impact; see *coalescence.*

accumulation: the part of the water cycle in which water collects on and in the earth.

acid rain: general term used for precipitation or fog that is more acidic than pure water.

advisories: statements issued by the National Weather Service giving information about significant weather conditions.

aerodynamic: shaped and smoothed to produce the least amount of resistance from the wind.

air mass: a large body of air that has similar characteristics of temperature and moisture over a large area.

air pollution: the contamination of the atmosphere with gases, chemicals, and particulate matter.

air quality: a measure of the cleanness of air.

anemometer: an instrument for measuring wind speed.

aneroid: a barometer without liquid.

barometer: an instrument for measuring atmospheric pressure.

biodegradable: something that breaks apart or decomposes due to the effects of temperature, water, and organisms.

calibration: the process of obtaining a standard frame of measurement.

ceiling: the height of the lowest layer of clouds which covers at least half of the sky.

climate: long-term weather conditions.

climatologists: scientists who study climate.

climograph: a climate graph showing temperature and rainfall values over a twelve-month period.

clouds: a collection of visible water and/or ice particles in the atmosphere; can also be a visible collection of particles such as dust or smoke.

coalescence: the merging of cloud droplets into a single larger droplet; see *accretion.*

cold front: the boundary along which a cold air mass pushes against a warm air mass.

condensation: the process by which water changes from gaseous to liquid form.

119

condensation nuclei: a particle, either liquid or solid, upon which condensation of water vapor begins in the atmosphere.

condensation trails (CONTRAILS): a high-altitude cloud that forms when hot, moist exhaust from an aircraft is quickly cooled.

conduction: the process of heat transfer by means of contact.

conductor: a substance that transfers heat by conduction easily.

convection: the process of transfer through up-and-down motions in the atmosphere.

converge: an atmospheric condition in which winds meet in a specific area.

Coriolis force: the deflective action observed on any free-moving object due to the Earth's rotation.

crepuscular rays: alternating light and dark bands of light (rays and shadows) that appear to fan out from the sun's position. These usually occur around sunrise and sunset and when the sun shines through breaks in a layer of clouds.

cyclone: another name for a low-pressure system; also the name given to tropical low-pressure systems in the Indian Ocean and near Australia.

data: information collected through observation or measurement for purposes of experimentation or analysis.

decompose: break apart or break down due to the action of weather, water, chemicals, or organisms.

degree-day: a measure of the departure of the average daily temperature from a given standard (usually 65°F); one degree-day is accumulated for each degree above or below the standard each day.

deposition: the process by which water vapor changes to ice without passing through an intermediate liquid stage.

dew: water that has condensed onto objects near the ground when their temperatures have fallen below the dew point of the adjacent air.

dew point temperature: as air cools, the temperature at which dew or condensation occurs.

Doppler radar: a radar system that measures not only precipitation intensity but also movement of precipitation toward and away from the radar.

downburst: a sudden localized rush of air downward within and beneath a thunderstorm.

erosion: the movement of soil or rock from one point to another by the action of the sea, running water, moving ice, precipitation, or wind; see *weathering.*

evaporation: the process by which water changes from a liquid to a gas.

extrapolation: forecasting future occurrences based on past data.

flooding: a situation in which water overflows the natural or artificial confines of a river or other water body.

freezing rain: rain that falls in liquid form but freezes upon impact to form a glaze upon the ground and exposed surfaces.

friction: a resisting force that acts to slow down the wind.

frost: during the cooling process, the formation of ice on exposed surfaces directly from water vapor.

geostationary: a satellite that orbits the Earth and remains at the same fixed point over the equator.

greenhouse effect: the process by which water vapor and carbon dioxide act to trap heat energy within the atmosphere.

hail: precipitation in the form of balls or irregularly shaped lumps of ice (ranging from pea-size to larger than a baseball) formed within cumulonimbus clouds.

halo: rings or arcs which encircle the sun or moon caused by bending of light passing through ice crystals (cirrus clouds).

high-pressure system: an area of high pressure around which the wind blows clockwise in the Northern Hemisphere.

humiture: an index which relates air temperature and relative humidity to how hot it feels.

hurricane: a severe tropical cyclone having winds greater than 74 mph (120 kph).

infrared: one type of energy emitted by objects which is not detectable by the human eye.

instability: a situation in which air easily moves vertically; usually refers to warmer air under cooler air.

insulator: a substance that prevents the transfer of heat by conduction.

isotherm: a line connecting points of equal temperature.

jet stream: a region of relatively strong winds concentrated within a narrow band in the atmosphere.

lightning: a visible electrical discharge produced by a thunderstorm.

low-pressure system: an area of low pressure around which the wind blows counterclockwise in the Northern Hemisphere.

mass: a measure of the amount of matter in an object.

meteorologist: a scientist who studies the atmosphere.

meteorology: study of the atmosphere and its interaction with the Earth and its life forms.

microburst: a small downburst.

precipitation: any form of water or ice particle which falls from the atmosphere and reaches the ground; see *virga.*

pressure: weight of air per unit area.

radar: an electronic instrument used for detecting and locating distant objects which scatter or reflect radio energy.

radiation: the process of heat transfer through air or space by wave-like energy emissions.

rain gauge: an instrument for measuring the amount of liquid precipitation.

reflect: to turn back a portion of the radiation that strikes an object.

relative humidity: the ratio of the amount of water vapor actually in the air compared to the amount of water vapor the air can hold at that temperature.

ridge: the top or crest of a wave.

runoff: the water, derived from precipitation that eventually reaches streams, rivers, lakes, and oceans.

satellite: something which orbits something else.

saturated: air that contains as much water vapor as it can hold at a given temperature.

sleet: small pellets of ice that form as rain falls through a layer of cold air.

snow core: a cylindrical sample of snow which, when melted, yields the snow's water content.

spectrum: a rainbowlike pattern produced when light passes through a prism and is split into its separate colors.

stability: a situation in which air resists vertical movement; usually refers to colder air underneath warmer air.

stationary front: a nonmoving boundary separating cold and warm air masses.

storm surge: an abnormal rise of the sea along a shore, primarily due to the winds of a storm, especially a hurricane.

sublimation: the process by which ice changes to water vapor without passing through an intermediate liquid stage.

sun dog: a colored spot produced by bending of light through ice crystals (cirrus clouds) that appears on either side of the sun.

temperature: a measure of the degree of hotness or coldness of a substance.

thermometer: an instrument for measuring temperature.

thunder: the sound caused when lightning rapidly heats air and causes it to expand.

thunderstorm: a local storm which contains thunder and lightning and is associated with cumulonimbus clouds.

tornado: a rapidly rotating column of air (often seen in the shape of a funnel or rope) extending from the bottom of a cumulonimbus cloud and touching the ground.

transpiration: the process by which water in plants is transferred as water vapor to the atmosphere.

tropical cyclones: a name given to all low-pressure systems in the tropics.

troposphere: the portion of the earth's atmosphere nearest the earth where most weather occurs; it extends from earth's surface to a height between 8 and 16 mi (5 to 10 km).

trough: the bottom or valley of a wave.

typhoon: the name given for a severe tropical cyclone in the western Pacific Ocean.

ultraviolet rays: one type of energy emitted by the sun which is not detectable by the human eye.

virga: precipitation which falls from a cloud but evaporates before reaching the ground; see *precipitation.*

warm front: the boundary along which a warm air mass pushes against a cold air mass.

warning: a statement issued by the National Weather Service that a particular dangerous weather event is likely to occur or is happening; it is a call to take action.

watch: a statement issued by the National Weather Service that a particular dangerous weather event may possibly occur in the near future; it is a caution to stay informed.

water cycle: the repetitive process by which water (in liquid, solid, and gaseous forms) moves through the earth-atmosphere-ocean system.

water vapor: water in its gaseous form.

wave: a pattern of up-and-down motions (undulations) in the atmosphere or in water.

weather: the condition of the atmosphere at any time and place.

weathering: the action by which rocks and soil are broken up by the effects of the sea, running water, moving ice, precipitation, or wind; see *erosion.*

weight: a measure of the heaviness of something.

wind: movement of air either horizontally or vertically.

windchill temperature: the combined cooling effect of temperature and wind on exposed skin.

wind vane: an instrument for measuring the direction from which the wind is blowing.

For Further Reading and Other Resources

BOOKS

Hart-Davis, Adam. *Scientific Eye.* New York: Sterling, 1989.

Herbert, Don. Mr. *Wizard's Supermarket Science.* New York: Random House, 1980.

Ludlum, David M. *The American Weather Book.* Boston: Houghton-Mifflin, 1982.

Ludlum, David M. *The Audubon Society Field Guide to North American Weather.* New York: Knopf, 1991.

Mandell, Muriel. *Simple Weather Experiments.* New York: Sterling, 1991.

Ontario Science Center. *Scienceworks.* Reading, Mass.: Addison-Wesley, 1984.

Pearce, E. A., and Smith, Gordon. *World Weather Guide.* New York: Times Books/Random House, 1990.

Walpole, Brenda. *175 Science Experiments to Amuse and Amaze Your Friends.* New York: Random House, 1988.

Williams, Jack. *The Weather Book.* New York: Random House, 1992.

MAGAZINES AND NEWSPAPERS

American Weather Observer: 401 Whitney Boulevard, Belvedere, IL 61008.

Weatherwise: Heldref Publishers, 1319 18th Street NW, Washington, DC 20036.

CLOUD CHARTS

How the Weatherworks: 1522 Baylor Avenue, Rockville, MD 20850.

WEATHER INSTRUMENTS AND SUPPLIES

Carolina Biological Supply Company: 2700 York Road, Burlington, NC 27215.

Edmund Scientific: 101 East Gloucester Pike, Barrington, NJ 08007-1380.

Frey Scientific: 905 Hickory Lane, Mansfield, OH 44905.

Index